MW00683240

RUNNING A FAMILY BUSINESS

Joseph R. Mancuso
and Nat Shulman

Debra DeSalvo, *Consulting Editor*

New York London Toronto Sydney Tokyo Singapore

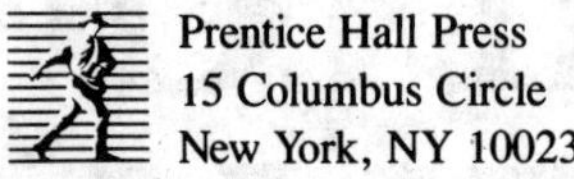
Prentice Hall Press
15 Columbus Circle
New York, NY 10023

Library of Congress Cataloging-in-Publication Data

Mancuso, Joseph R.
Running a family business / Joseph R. Mancuso and Nat Shulman.
p. cm.
Includes index.
ISBN 0-13-784026-8
1. Family-owned business enterprises—Management. 2. Work and family. I. Shulman, Nat. II. Title.
HD62.25.M36 1991
658.02′2—dc20 90-26545
CIP

Designed by Irving Perkins Associates

Manufactured in the United States of America

10 9 8 7 6 5 4 3 2 1

First Edition

ACKNOWLEDGMENTS

I want to thank all the families who came to the CEO Club's three-day Family Business experience at the top of the mountain to share ideas. Without their generous input, many of the ideas in this book would not have gelled. As Nat and I like to say, "It's okay to be independent, but there is no reason to be alone."

We both thank Ed and Darlene Lowe of Kitty Litter fame for sharing their 3,000-acre Big Rock Valley farm in Cassopolis, Michigan, with all of us. This lovely and unique setting provided the perfect place for meandering and pondering, which is the country version of management by wandering around. It's a special place.

—Joseph R. Mancuso, New York City

To Sandra Celli and Dick Caravati of the DMA Group, Exeter, New Hampshire, whose wise counsel and guidance during the research for this book was invaluable.

To my children, Scott, Karen, and Ronald, who were star players in our family business experience and demonstrated patience and tolerance with a high-powered entrepreneur who found letting go a problem.

And finally, to my wife, Corky, for encouragement and support during my transition from an entrepreneur to a writer.

—Nat Shulman, Boston

Contents

Introduction: When Families Meet Businesses

When Joe Mancuso, entrepreneur extraordinaire, met Nat Shulman, a career new car dealer and aspiring writer who had experienced successorship in a family business from both sides of the table, a child was born—a book child. After more than three years of presenting workshops to Mancuso's vast network of CEO Clubs from New York to L.A. plus several intensive three-day Family Business Experiences at Ed and Darlene Lowe's farm in Cassopolis, Michigan, Mancuso and Shulman decided to share this valuable information. Hence this book.

Previous family business books have dealt with estate tax issues and how to handle the legal distribution of assets after the demise or retirement of the family business owner. But our experiences in family businesses indicate the legal and tax issues are generally well taken care of by most family business owners. The most glaring deficiency—and the subject most often overlooked in previous family business books—was the manner in which family members were "beating up on each other" within the business, causing irreparable damage to the family unit and its members (not to mention having a negative effect on the business, its stockholders, employees, suppliers, and—most important—its customers).

Consider the families within your circle who are involved in family businesses. How many horror stories can you recall where family members clashed over personality issues, resulting in the family's breaking apart? On a national scale, take a look at the Binghams of Kentucky, the former publishers of the

Louisville Courier, where both family and business were torn asunder by family members who couldn't get along in the workplace. Or the Kirbys, whose grandfather cofounded the F. W. Woolworth Company in 1930 and who are currently threatening to dismantle the Alleghany Corporation. Kirby siblings own 39 percent of the stock and have already destroyed any vestige of a Kirby family. The *New York Times* refers to the squabble as "intense and venomous," while a Kirby family member refers to the action of a sibling as "disloyal, sneaky, and dishonest."

The issues may often be financial in that stockholders may not be receiving what they consider an adequate cash return on their stock. However, our research shows that serious discord in family businesses is often caused by misguided expectations and invalid assumptions by family members working in the business.

This book is meant to be, more than anything else, a guide to help families get along successfully in the family business, while also running a successful, profitable business operation.

1. Copreneurs: Entrepreneurial Couples

Sharan and Frank Barnett

> For far too many of us, employment controls our lives, uprooting us from our communities and isolating us from families and friends.
>
> Copreneuring is one way to regain positive control of our lives and become personally responsible for our futures.

Copreneuring is based on equality, mutual trust, a shared vision for the enterprise, a high degree of communication, and a lack of interpersonal competition. It reflects a lifestyle that incorporates the work and personal worlds. Our intention is not to introduce another term to the already overstocked arsenal of business terminology, yet our research has uncovered a new social and economic phenomenon that simply called out for its own appellation.

It is our dream to have couples working together as equals, and that couples who had not previously considered copreneuring will be stimulated by the possibility.

An End to Separate Lives and Agendas

Often we find ourselves in employment that brings us little personal satisfaction, autonomy, or joy. To compensate for the sense of emptiness arising from the separation of our personal and work lives, one response has been to fill the void with material goods. However, they are a sorely inadequate substitute for the bonds of human contact that many of us have lost.

Today a new wave of entrepreneurs is showing a new way to regain the values of gentler times. These dynamic individuals have developed a modern version of an age-old economic unit—the family—and are showing us a way to return to independence and the security of self-reliance.

Copreneurial Enterprise—A New Branch of the Family Business Tree

Cultural changes, or "runoff," have altered our society since family businesses were first examined in the United States—the struggle for equal rights for women, the decimation of the nuclear family, the development of a highly individualistic society, the preponderance of two-income, dual-career families, and the loss of a sense of community. When investigating the copreneurial movement, we concluded we were identifying a new branch of the family business tree—copreneurial enterprises.

By definition, copreneurial ventures are a form of family business. Yet unlike orthodox family businesses, copreneurs make a commitment to a shared lifestyle rather than to building an empire to pass on to future generations. Copreneurs are dream builders who mold their personal and working worlds into expressions of their own unique visions.

The journey from that time when we were copreneurs in our first business venture together to being viewed as one of the nation's most vocal proponents of the copreneurial movement has been a fascinating voyage. We have confirmed that copreneurs face issues very different from those of traditional family businesses.

The single hot topic in virtually every family business is succession. Running a close second, third, and fourth are the issues of family dynamics, the integration of nonfamily members into the business, and breakdowns in communication between family members.

So little is understood about the distinctions between copreneurial enterprises and traditional family businesses that the issue of succession continues to be presented to copreneurs who, more often than not, do not expect or even desire their children to succeed them in business.

Of course, many copreneurial enterprises will undoubtedly be transformed into true family businesses as the enterprise passes on to the next generation. However, that first wave of entrepreneurial pioneers we call copreneurs did not establish their businesses with the intent to pass them on as a legacy for their children—they founded their ventures out of a desire to gain control over their own lives and to work together.

Although other family members often participate as employees in copreneurial enterprises, they are not involved because the founders believe their children should work in their company. Rather, children who work in these businesses do so because of the contribution they can make to the venture—not necessarily because their parents own the business. To copreneurs, it is more important that they *empower* their children with the ability to control their own lives than to expect them to follow their parents' dreams. After all, their children have dreams of their own.

Rather than succession, copreneurs choose to sell their businesses, take them public, or simply to close the doors when they are ready to move on together to another venture or to retire.

Joe Mancuso's wife Karla's parents are an example of this phenomenon. Margaret-Ann and Karl Schulz (Karla is named after her dad) owned and operated several five-and-ten-cent stores in a little town in Wisconsin. They ran this business as a lifestyle for almost forty years. They had no intention of either of their two daughters ever taking over the enterprise.

The Schulzes sold the business in 1984 and started another business together as a franchised real estate firm in the same little town. To them, working together in a small town in a confined space was a joy, and all they wanted from the business.

Today, Joe and Karla Mancuso have worked together for more than a decade. Joe believes the reason their business and personal relationship has prospered has a great deal to do with how Karla saw her parents prosper when she was a child.

THE PARADOX OF COPRENEURING

The clashes over conflicting values, the sibling rivalries, and the complex psychological issues prevalent in many family businesses are often absent in copreneurial enterprises. However, horror stories of the "perils" of spouses working together make good copy for the media while propagating the myth that copreneuring is not only unhealthy for personal relationships but that it also spells long-term disaster for any enterprise. Not that some horror stories aren't true—the struggle of the San Francisco–based E'spirit Company to survive was, in large part, negatively affected by the deterioration of the husband–wife team, whose frequent altercations were constantly reported in the newspapers.

But for the most part, couples who work together have found that it is a great way to be entrepreneurial. And this is the paradox of copreneuring—though many prejudge (without trying it) that it will be a complete failure on a personal and a financial level, it is usually a success on both.

Copreneuring and Its Unique Value System

Of the copreneurs we talked with, very few reported that they had established their enterprise with the primary objective of getting rich or making a fast buck. Rather, the formation of these businesses represents a commitment to a lifestyle in which the relationship between the partners is an integral part of the whole, and in which personal security is not necessarily defined by the wealth those businesses can generate. The many couples running country inns in Vermont are examples of these values.

It isn't the money that drives copreneurs—it's the gratification they receive from working together. Many of these enterprises provide services to the community that focus on environmental or social issues, while others provide social services, such as on-site day care, for their employees. Copreneuring involves not only a commitment to a particular enterprise; it reflects a lifestyle that unifies the world of work with the worlds of family and community.

Copreneuring is a very personal response addressing those economic and social factors that have emerged since World War II and are directly linked to the growing social problems our country faces today. We find copreneurial businesses have been founded on *values* rather than *drives*—values centered on good human relations and social responsibility in contrast with competitive drives centered on individual achievement and a self-centered, never-ending quest for economic gain.

Copreneurs seek to integrate drives and values holistically into their lives. No longer do drives and values need to exist in the separate realms of work and of family and intimacy. Copreneurs are showing us the way to integrate the family, love, and work, and in the process are redefining the parameters of sharing power.

There is, after all, something wholesome and natural about a couple working together. Their persona is more complete than that normally presented by management in the world of work. Copreneuring is a unique model for businesses and management—it offers unlimited opportunities for expanding upon mutual strengths and dependencies, while the traditional business model is often closed and self-serving.

Couples working together run counter to America's love affair with rugged individualism and our culture's reverence for the lone entrepreneur. In the final analysis, entrepreneurs working in isolation are a reflection of two characteristics of our postwar society—our competitive individualism and our inability to work together. Copreneuring is a positive sign of our times and a healthy personal and economic response to an otherwise isolating workplace.

"I Was Working Late at the Office"

A business can be very demanding. If either partner in the copreneurial businesses we explored had established and maintained their enterprise as an entrepreneur rather than as a copreneur, his or her personal life would have been greatly affected. Many entrepreneurs whose spouses are not involved in their business acknowledge that the pressures of the enterprise, along with the extraordinarily long hours required to launch and run a successful business, can place strains upon personal relationships that escalate to the breaking point.

Copreneurs are entrepreneurs who never need to go home and explain to an uninvolved spouse what's going on at work. The inevitable late hours, setbacks, and losses (as well as the discoveries and triumphs) are all understood and shared equally between these partners. Moreover, these copreneurs brainstorm and discuss problems and opportunities spontaneously, receiving instant feedback. The spontaneity with which these couples operate can allow their businesses to change and respond to market needs quickly and efficiently.

The synergism between two intimate partners can be truly dynamic. It is astounding what a single human being can accomplish alone, but these adventurous couples have proven that two can accomplish far more together than the sum of each working separately.

Knowing When It's Right to Work Together

When we, the Barnetts, first started working together, we were often confronted with the observation that it must be difficult for a husband and wife to work together day in and day out, remain friends, and function as individual professionals in the competitive business world.

The fascination expressed by so many toward our partnership prompted us to reexamine our own personal and working lives. We knew we had discovered almost from the beginning a collective strength far beyond our individual capabilities. In a society based on independence—even within personal relationships—our choice had been to merge all aspects of our lives.

Our decision to work together as partners evolved as a process. We were fortunate to have been best friends before deciding to form our own company. One of our principal assets was having had the opportunity to "test the waters" by working together for other firms before striking out on our own as copreneurs. We quickly discovered we were more creative and productive collectively than when working apart. Many of the copreneurs we met shared similar stories of testing the waters by gaining employment as a team before founding their own enterprise.

How does a couple know when working together is right for them? The answer to this seemingly complex question is, in fact, deceptively simple—the couple who *cannot* work together is the first to acknowledge it would be impossible for them. They are the ones who say, "I could *never, never* work with my spouse!" And yet for the couple entertaining the notion of working together, the leap from dream to reality is based on the knowledge that they are *already* working cooperatively as a team in many areas of their personal lives—as comanagers of the business aspects of running a household, as financial planners for their family's future, as parents, and as partners in often-taxing and complex projects such as building or remodeling a house.

In the foreword to our book, *Working Together: Entrepreneurial Couples,* Ian and Betty Ballantine, who have worked together for nearly fifty years, wrote, "There is this idiotic myth that husband and wife cannot, indeed perhaps should not, work together, as though working would threaten their personal relationship. The truth is, we probably could not have succeeded in either endeavor—marriage or work—without the support of the other activity. Each of us is a strong-minded individual with a need to concentrate interest with function. Had our career objectives been widely divergent, we would probably have had to go our separate ways since neither of us would have the time for, or interest in, the activities of the other."

The Ballantines wrote of their own experiences as leaders in America's book publishing industry, first bringing Penguin Books to this country before World War II and later founding Ballantine Books, a venture in which there were three other sets of married partners all working together.

As this couple learned and proved so successfully in a shared career spanning nearly five decades, there is far less chemistry or mystery to working together than we have been led to believe. They would also surely agree that there is no litmus test with which couples can determine their "copreneurial aptitude."

However, in spite of the lack of any clear test, there *is* a process couples go through when considering working together. The process begins when the couple first makes a commitment to their relationship. That commitment may or may not include the possibility that the marriage partners can or will want to become business partners. But we have learned that the phases of relationships that couples go through weed out those individuals whose relationships could not survive the strain of running a business.

Dr. Dennis Jaffe, who works with his wife, Dr. Cynthia Scott, in the HeartWork Group, a consulting firm they cofounded in San Francisco, holds the view that "It just may be that copreneurs are more successful than a corresponding group of entrepreneurs." Dr. Jaffe finds that "Copreneurs tend to be a hardy bunch of entrepreneurs. Beginning with the structural nature of getting a personal relationship to work, followed by taking on the risk and strains of a new venture, plus the added companionship and pressure, I don't think a fragile couple would take this on. The nature of copreneuring scares them off, just as the nature of starting a business frightens otherwise talented people. In addition, the special strengths of an effective couple relationship are especially useful in resolving the pressures of starting a company."

Dr. Jaffe further contends: "The relationship of the copreneurs has to be strong, flexible, egalitarian, and relatively free of deep, basic conflicts. It is helpful if the couple has had positive experiences of working together. Perhaps planning large events or a project like building a new house. If they enjoy working together, and are able to work together with free sharing of ideas and give-and-take, then they are ready for shared work. The relationship should not be one where one person habitually bows to the will of the other, or does not feel free to speak up."

We have also discovered that, contrary to the common wisdom that the logical order for establishing a business begins with the discovery of a needed product or service, many copreneurs begin with the decision to work together and then proceed "backward" to the discovery of exactly what it is they will do together.

The remarkable story of Ted and Joyce Rice, cofounders of T. J. Cinnamons, the nation's largest bakery franchise company, began in 1982 when the couple took a three-month sabbatical from their respective careers. That time out from their busy lives allowed them to reflect and examine their future. At the end of the three months, the Rices had reached the conclusion that they could do anything they wanted—even start their own business. And they agreed that regardless of the nature of their new venture, it would have to allow them to work together.

After exploring businesses from delicatessens to craft shops, they were struck with the idea of a bakery specializing in cinnamon rolls. Ted spent the next winter designing a twenty-foot mobile bakery. Meanwhile, Joyce designed the now-famous eight-ounce, softball-sized gourmet cinnamon roll. And a new chapter began in their incredible success story.

Although we do not believe an actual checklist through which couples can *discover* their copreneurial compatibility can or needs to be devised, both individuals within the relationship must have a solid grasp of their own capabilities and weaknesses and both must be committed to working together. To be copreneurial is not to meld two incomplete individuals into one whole entity—it is to gain a new third "self" when two whole individuals join forces.

My Brain, Your Brain, and Our Brain

In the early months of working together, we quickly recognized we are a potent team. When we accomplished a particularly difficult task or met one more "impossible" deadline, we would quip to each other, "Between us we have one great brain."

Once we realized that working together allowed us to maximize our talents and minimize our weaknesses, we came to understand that because of our working relationship, we were each operating at a full 100 percent. Together we are more than the sum of our separate parts—not 200 percent, but 300 percent. When couples work together, one plus one really does equal three!

The synergism between us has resulted in a magnification of our combined abilities. Every project we have completed has clearly been the product of more than just the two of us. Our creations are the result of the synergy that we refer to fondly as *our brain*.

That same synergism is at the disposal of all copreneurs, making it possible for couples working together to accomplish "the impossible." It is uncanny how couple after couple refers to this phenomenon and acknowledges how they rely on it. Often, copreneurs allude to a "third entity" or "person" that exists somewhere between them. That *being* is so very real to us that in the dedication to our book we wrote, "We dedicate this book to that strange and wonderful entity that seems to reside somewhere between every entrepreneurial couple. It is not *him*, it is not *her*, and it is much more than *them*."

To Specialize or Not to Specialize

For most couples, the division of labor comes quite naturally as a result of individual capabilities, knowledge, skills, and what each partner brings to the venture from their past.

Generally, the couples we interviewed used individual capabilities and skills as their primary criteria for role assumption, rather than adopting stereotypic roles associated with masculinity or femininity. These were enterprises in which both partners appeared to be equally powerful. And yet in many of these businesses the female partner had begun without any previous entrepreneurial activity—in some cases without management experience, or even knowledge specific to the new endeavor. Some of these women had been housewives or employed in unchallenging positions that offered little hope for personal growth or career advancement. We should note that a similar lack of knowledge or experience specific to their new enterprise did not deter the male half of some partnerships, either.

Traditionally, women have not been allowed to assume active control when men are on the scene. Although capable of assuming full responsibility for virtually any situation, women have been expected to relinquish control and responsibility when men are present. However, this traditional model was not encountered among the entrepreneurial couples we met.

In couple after couple, we found strong women who have emerged as savvy and influential forces within their organizations and industries. Behind every great female copreneur, we discovered a strong male counterpart. The men in these relationships were not only able to recognize and draw upon the strengths of their partners, they also possessed self-images that could not be threatened either personally or professionally by their partner's success and growth. These copreneurial men did not wrest the helm from their partner, but instead shared the navigation and control of their business equally.

One of the first major decisions copreneurs will face is to choose the working style best suited to both partners. This involves one basic decision—to work together, sharing tasks and responsibilities, or to divide the elements of the business and work on them separately. Therefore, copreneurs must decide whether their working style will be one of specialization by determining which of these styles is best suited to their personal abilities, relationship, and enterprise.

Extending the Boundaries of Mutual Dependency

When Nick and Liz Thomas, who for many years had prepared batches of mustard as Christmas gifts from an old family recipe, founded Chalif, Inc., they came to the realization that their business would be more than just a cottage industry. Within weeks of the initial sales of their delicious mustard, Joe Mancuso, a close friend, called with an attractive financial proposal that included a partnership in their enterprise.

The couple's immediate response was to reject the offer, saying, "Oh, no, Joe, we're not going to give up part of our company." However, Joe was insistent. "I know Nick has experience in the management of the business, but he doesn't know anything about a start-up company. Let me help you."

With that, Liz and Nick began four months of weekly meetings with Joe, who later became their partner. In the meantime, reorders were coming in and the Thomases were scrambling to keep up. Nick had no time to find new accounts, and their revenues were immediately reinvested into the ingredients to keep their mustard in the stores. It didn't take long to recognize they would have to move their business out of their home to increase production and to resume family life on a normal schedule. This realization also meant that setting up a manufacturing facility would take additional capital. It became obvious that Liz and Nick needed a front man. They finally took Joe up on his offer and for his initial investment gave him 30 percent of the company.

Today, Joe sits on the board of directors of the corporation, but allows Nick and Liz a completely free rein in the operation of their highly successful business that manufactures and sells gourmet mustards and condiments nationwide. Since Joe isn't a working partner, the Thomases keep him abreast of everything. The couple understands what it takes to make a partnership work—friendship, explicit trust, mutual respect, and free-flowing open communication. And most important, neither Nick, Liz, nor Joe had an ego that got in the way of the partnership or required taking absolute control.

Without their partner, getting Chalif, Inc. off the ground might have been more than the Thomases could have managed. With Joe's participation, their gourmet mustard quickly went on to gain national recognition and distribution, moving from their kitchen to an 8,400-square-foot plant in Wyndmoor, Pennsylvania.

Extending Open and Supportive Management Style to Employees

Because copreneuring is based on trust, equality, sharing, and a lack of interpersonal competition between the husband and wife founders, communication is the key ingredient in every successful copreneurial relationship and business. This high degree of communication flows not only between the copreneurs but between them and their employees as well.

Many copreneurs have demonstrated that it is possible to manage employees in a style that uses the same valuable tools—freedom from interpersonal competition, communication, trust, and shared objectives—that have allowed their copreneurial relationship to flourish.

Since a remarkable percentage (nearly two-thirds) of the couples we interviewed began their enterprises right in their homes, many brought employees into that setting as well. When employees are brought into a home-based business, it is quite natural for an informal atmosphere to prevail.

If a business remains home-based, the informality between founders and employees will continue. And as is most often the case, when an enterprise moves into a more traditional business setting, the camaraderie and sense of togetherness between the owners and the original staff will continue as the business grows. While those original staff members remain with the company, that early kinship continues as a part of the work setting, and through them it can flow down to newer employees as they join the team.

Copreneuring provides a unique opportunity to develop a management style characterized by close interactions between owners and staff and the nurturance and support of employees. The foundation of copreneuring is teamwork and because of the success of the copreneurial relationship, many copreneurs do not hire just employees—they hire team members.

Copreneurs Turn Egos into Wegos

In a partnership based on trust, there is no need to prove oneself right or the other wrong. Individual egos merge into *wegos*—a combined ego, shared noncompetitively by the partners and directed constructively outside the relationship.

We do not suggest partners place their egos on hold or attempt to rein them in. Rather, we believe strong egos are necessary in any entrepreneurial venture and two egos blended into one wego can be powerful.

The blending of two distinct egos can't be expected to occur overnight. But once blended, the resulting wego is very different from the individual egos from which it evolved. One by-product of this blending of egos is the demise of self-centered competition between partners.

At the center of the ego is "I, myself—number one." A fully developed wego, on the other hand, focuses on "we, ourselves," placing the emphasis on the relationship and the enterprise rather than on the individual. A wego evolves with the realization that both partners are contributing 100 percent to their venture. It comes with the pride of knowing that together you've accomplished your goal—not with the statement "I'm proud of it because I did it," but rather, "I'm proud of it because *we* did it."

Wegos evolve out of the self-confidence of each partner acknowledging that together they possess the individual capabilities to achieve their goals and the realization that without *ourselves,* the concept of *myself* is meaningless.

A wego, by its very nature, must be free of the self-importance of a single competitive individual, and focused on the interdependence of the relationship between equal partners. It must blend those behaviors once deemed to reside exclusively in one or the other sexes. To share possession of a wego is to feel totally human and whole in both your work and personal lives.

Business Is Business—You Can't Take It Personally

Perhaps the most common misperception concerning couples working together is expressed by the following statement: "How can you work together all the time without fighting? If we were together that much, we'd be at each other's throats day and night!" This view is based on the assumption that anger between individuals is unhealthy and destructive, and therefore it would be unhealthy and destructive to work together because the more couples are together, the more they will fight.

Anger, like love, has an enormous capacity for fostering positive change and growth. There is a difference between anger and the *uncontrolled* expression of deep emotion. Anger can be used for destructive purposes or it can be a building block of communication, and communication is the foundation of every healthy relationship. Anger is a *process,* not a disease; it has a cause and a result. The only way to deal with your own anger is to express it honestly.

Because of the trust and commitment between couples who work together, copreneurs know that when disagreements, problems, or arguments arise, their relationship is not in jeopardy. When both partners are strong individuals, disagreements and anger should be anticipated as an essential part of the process of working together.

As action-driven individuals, copreneurs believe the cause of arguments is not of primary importance. They understand the task between them is not just to arrive at a mutual understanding of "Why anger?"; what's important is an appropriate course of action in response to the problem, and to follow it through.

Anger can be a spark for communication and enlightenment, but resolution requires the participation of both partners. Work at it together. Arguments alone do not resolve problems, but they *can* lead to understanding the other's point of view, which is often necessary in reaching a solution. It is what happens after the argument is over that is important. We firmly believe that if you and your partner don't argue and disagree on occasion, you are not *really* communicating. They say that fights between two alley cats just seem to produce more alley cats.

The Family Juggling Act

Copreneurs must come to terms with the juggling act of balancing their families, their homes, their enterprises, and whatever time may be left over for a social life and personal interests. You can't reasonably expect to put in twelve to sixteen hours a day at work, prepare lavish meals, maintain a meticulous house and a gracious style of living, and still have time for personal activities and relaxation without some outside assistance. Coming to this realization is not easy, especially for the women in copreneurial relationships. Liz Thomas of Chalif, Inc. described the quandary she found herself confronting as their business grew:

"I had not resolved my career versus my nurturing role at home. It was a real identity crisis and it had to do with my trying to be Superwife, Supermother, and Superexecutive, without any time left for me. It came at a time when we were understaffed and I was trying to do everything at work and at home. I didn't have any time for *me,* and it was something I had to learn—that it's important for everybody else's welfare that I am able to take care of myself as well. No one else was putting the pressure on me to be perfect—I was doing it to myself!"

Balancing the world of work with the demands at home is one of the greatest challenges that an entrepreneurial couple will encounter. It goes without saying that there are not enough hours in each day to accomplish all that needs to be done at work, let alone in a busy household.

As Liz realized, the first hurdle to overcome is psychological. Women, in particular, have difficulty relinquishing control of the household and accepting compromises in the home. They and their families must learn to compromise and set priorities on what has to be done, what someone else can do, and what they can live without doing.

As the twentieth century draws to a close, dealing with organizational problems at home is emerging as a major issue for copreneurs and dual-income households. For working parents today, mothers and fathers alike, there is a "second shift" of tasks that must be attended to before the workday begins and upon returning home following the trials and tribulations of the workplace. In spite of the gains in equality that women have achieved in the world of work, the second shift falls largely on their shoulders. In many marriages, it is this second shift that chafes at a relationship—often to the point of tearing it apart.

As Arlie Hochschild wrote in her book, *The Second Shift: Working Parents and the Revolution at Home* (Viking Penguin, 1989), "In one study of 600 couples filing for divorce, researcher George Levinger found that the second most common reason women cited for wanting to divorce—after 'mental cruelty'—was their husbands' 'neglect of home or children.' " Women mentioned this reason more often than financial problems, physical abuse, drinking, or infidelity.

Women, according to Dr. Hochschild, work roughly fifteen more hours each week than men—that's an extra month of twenty-four-hour days each year, and over a dozen years, it adds up to one full year of grueling household toil. Even when a couple does not have children, women, perhaps not surprisingly, still devote significantly more time than their spouses to housework. "Just as there is a wage gap between men and women in the workplace," Dr. Hochschild observes, "there is a 'leisure gap' between them at home."

In a survey we conducted of copreneurs across the nation in early 1990, we asked couples to rank their individual participation by percentage of involvement in the following categories:

1. Personal finances
2. Housekeeping
3. Child care
4. Cooking
5. Laundry
6. Household shopping
7. Home maintenance
8. Gardening
9. Planning family activities and events
10. The social calendar

Typically, the only areas of activity dominated by males were in the categories of home maintenance and gardening. As a rule, in all areas of household responsibilities there was only token participation by men—even in the day-to-day care of their own children. Copreneurs, like dual-career couples, must come to grips with the inequality that remains in their personal lives.

For most copreneurs, finding the time to socialize or just get away from their business can present a real problem, especially when the business is young or experiencing growth and expansion. Because of the extremely close nature of their personal relationships, some couples seem not to seek out or to miss the company of friends. Many entrepreneurial couples have learned to balance their busy professional lives with a rich social calendar, while others clearly long for the time when the demands of their enterprise will diminish and allow them to resume an active social life.

While finding the time to socialize can be a challenge for many copreneurs, structuring vacations into busy schedules sometimes presents an even greater dilemma. Consequently, entrepreneurial couples learn to make the most of any business trip, often scheduling time for relaxation into their itinerary or including the family in their business travels. Joe and Karla Mancuso are a good example of this phenomenon. For the past six years, as a copreneurial couple they have conducted a minimum of eight meetings in eight CEO Club chapters. That's a minimum of sixty-four meetings annually. In fact, it's close to 150 meetings annually. They have traveled together (bringing along Max, their captivating three-year-old infant son) to each of these meetings, often arriving early and leaving late. They regard these CEO Club meetings in San Francisco, Los Angeles, Dallas, Chicago, Boston, Washington, DC, and Pittsburgh as a continual vacation. Otherwise, it would be hard work!

Children of copreneurs are likely to be highly knowledgeable and involved in their parents' enterprises. They are exposed to the business over the breakfast and dinner tables, and often participate in business functions and social events. Many copreneurs recognize that their children have valuable insights and can make often amazing contributions. However, children can become bored with the constant stream of business talk that occupies so much of their parents' conversation and can even come to feel a "sibling rivalry" with the enterprise.

Knowing When to Quit

A couple should know when the time is right to let go of their business altogether. It is wise to have a plan for leaving the business behind almost from the very beginning of a venture. And while it may seem strange to develop a contingency plan for severing the ties to your own business at the outset, many enterprises are founded with the goal of eventually being sold.

Copreneurs should be aware of the circumstances when getting out of their business is the most appropriate thing to do—if the world is knocking at the door with offers to buy them out; if the big guys become their competition and begin to overpower them with heavy marketing and advertising dollars; or if retirement is drawing near and the couple needs to diversify their investments. And copreneurs need to look objectively at their enterprise and accept the sometimes devastating reality that all their hard work, commitment, and belief in their venture will not lead to success—no matter how much time, energy, or financial resources they have already invested or are willing to commit in the future. At those painful moments of realization, the couple must remember it is the health of the *relationship* they share that must come first.

A couple should not feel that their enterprise need live on forever. As long as it is serving the needs for which it was founded, and as long as the founders are enjoying running the business, selling out or just closing the doors should not be a consideration. But if a couple finds themselves in constant conflict with each other over business matters, or if the thrill of business is gone for the two of them, then it may be time to start investigating alternatives—including ending their participation in the enterprise.

Copreneuring Is the Future

If you are considering breaking away from the traditional world of work and starting a business, we feel that you can find no better partner than your spouse, significant other, or however you define that special relationship—*your best friend*. We make this recommendation with the knowledge that copreneuring is not for every couple.

As we approach the new millennium, copreneurs in increasing numbers are regaining control of their work worlds as well as their personal lives. These couples are successfully blending those two realms, the work and the personal, into a harmonious whole and are showing us one path out of an economic way of life that undermines many of our most basic psychological and emotional needs. Copreneuring is an end to separate lives and separate agendas.

The self-made man has always been an American cultural ideal. Today, the self-made couple is a personal response to a changing economic and social climate. During this decade, copreneurial enterprises will emerge in ever-increasing numbers. One year after the publication of our book, the World Future Society published a special report, "Outlook '90—And Beyond," that highlighted seventy-one forecasts ranging from world affairs and transportation to health, work, and the family. Among these glimpses into the near future, the Society predicted that "Married couples who work together—copreneurs—may be the wave of America's business future."

Copreneurs are people who are in control of their lives, doing work they love, and doing it with the one they love. As one copreneur told us, "In the long run, we're sharing the burden equally. And no matter how tough it is to put your head on the pillow at night because you're worried, the other person putting their head on the pillow is equally worried, or equally proud, or equally elated. Our relationship has matured much faster because we've worked together."

Working together is a great way for people to have relationships—and it's a great way for people to be entrepreneurial. We recommend it to everyone. Copreneuring is the future.

Guidelines for Transforming Anger into a Powerful Communications Tool

1. Express Anger with Anger. When you experience anger, make sure what you are angry about is a *real* issue. If it is, express it openly and honestly.

2. Identify the Issue. Very often, people feel anger without being able to identify its cause. Learn the source of your anger and deal with your emotion as if it were a concrete object. Once you know the cause of your anger, you can work on its resolution.
3. Listen to the Meaning Behind the Words. You will have to listen carefully, "reading between the lines," to discover the origin of your partner's unhappiness. Ask questions, and if the real cause of anger is not clear, take the time to explore together what it could be. Questions are the key to listening. Ask, don't tell.
4. Deal with Anger as Quickly as Possible. Whether you choose privacy or public confrontation, deal with your anger quickly and completely and get it over with. Above all, don't hold a grudge or keep score. Remember, you are *both* on the same team and *each* of you is one-half of the partnership. Like Siamese twins, there is no winner or loser.
5. Keep on Track. Stick to the current problem. Don't dredge up old feelings or issues. Live in the present, but learn from the past. We call that "throwing in the kitchen sink." Avoid tactics that will obstruct your progress toward resolution, such as name-calling or verbal blows that you know will hit a sensitive nerve. Those are the destroyers.
6. Put Yourself in Your Partner's Place. It always helps to understand the other person's point of view. Because copreneurs are two individuals, there will always be two views of every issue. When you wear your partner's shoes, you will be better able to understand that other point of view. To resolve an issue, you must deal with all its aspects. Understanding your partner can bring you closer together.
7. Fight Fair. A no-holds-barred approach to disagreements can be destructive. Anger is a moral emotion that can be used to right a wrong or correct an injustice. It is also a communication tool that can help you both grow together.
8. Don't Be Afraid to Use Humor. In fact, it's like conflict penicillin! When you begin to see the absurdity of an argument, and feel the corners of your mouth itching to smile, let it happen. *Shared* laughter is nature's finest balm to soothe frayed tempers. Interjecting humor during the heat of a disagreement can be tricky business. But if it's sincere and not aimed at your partner, it's worth a try. And if you are willing to personally become the butt of the humor, then the conflict is over and you've both won.
9. Learn from Your Mistakes and Move On. Experience is the best teacher. When you discover you've made a mistake, learn quickly from it, ac-

knowledge it freely, and go on with the business at hand. Don't spend excess time on *mea culpas*. Let go of past mistakes with the resolution not to repeat them.

10. Never Withdraw or Build Walls. Withdrawing and building emotional barriers can be used as an offensive as well as defensive weapon. If you retreat into solitude, agreement and resolution with your partner will be impossible.

2. Sons and Daughters

The Obsession with "Being Fair"

The foremost question in the mind of the family business owner who is about to bring children into the business or address the challenges of estate planning is: "Am I distributing my assets and providing opportunity in the family business in a fair and equitable manner for *all* my kids?"

This obsession with being fair stems from love—is ethically and morally admirable—and can play havoc with the operation of your business and your succession plans. "Being fair" can damage a family business in many ways. Here are some examples:

- An incompetent family member is placed in a senior management position, simply because a competent sibling earned a similar position.
- A "fair" will forces a talented and involved son or daughter to share senior management decisions with passive sibling stockholders. These stockholders, who may be dependent upon their cash dividends, force short-term cash disbursements that damage the long-term health of the firm.
- Concern that children and grandchildren be treated "fairly" compels the senior head of the business to appoint in-laws to critical management positions so they can enforce "fairness."
- Competent, ambitious female family members are innocently overlooked as

successor candidates while the "old man," suffering from archaic sex bias, seeks to push the business onto incompetent and uninterested sons.

- Fearful of being labeled "unfair," the owner of a thriving business delays declaring who will be in charge should he suddenly die or become disabled—leaving the business wide open to damaging power struggles should something actually happen to him.
- Loyal and talented long-term managers are ignored as potential buy-out owners in order to keep the business in the hands of significantly less capable family members.

A family business is a money pump that can usually benefit an entire family for many years as long as the person operating the pump is competent. What the kids should get out of the business is money—plain and simple. Therefore, if you want to be genuinely fair, choose managers and successors who can produce profits. Selling the business to a loyal, valued manager and giving the kids income-producing stock may be fairer than allowing misguided decisions based on love and guilt to run the company into the ground. Never let the operational control of the family business become more important to you or your family than the quality of the bottom line. The annals of family business failures are filled with tales of incompetent family members thrust into management positions upon the untimely death of the owner—even when competent nonfamily managers were readily available within the organization to preserve the business. In short, the heck with being fair when it comes to the operational control of the business: Be fair with the real estate and the money instead.

A Family Business Saga

In nonfamily-affiliated businesses, new employees usually have no history of interaction with management beyond the job interview. They start work with a clean slate, and their future with the company depends only on their talent, the company's prosperity, and their ability to get along with people in the workplace. Their family life is confidential unless they choose to share it. During the sensitive employment trial period, no long-term personal attachments cloud the objectivity of their superiors.

The son or daughter of the boss coming to work in the family business for the first day should be so lucky! Here's an illustration of how a father/owner and his son might interact through four decades in the family business:

1946 Twenty-five-year-old Dad is looking for a career, and his family begins with the birth of Junior.

1951 Dad is finding that he's an aggressive entrepreneur, and he begins to dream about owning his own business. Junior, the apple of his eye, is about to start public school.

1956 At age thirty-five, Dad's dream is realized! Purchase, sale, and loan agreements are signed—with the personal guarantees required for the loans putting all personal assets of the young family at risk. Dad gets to work, and both the risks and the potential rewards prompt him to keep working twelve-hour days with increased zeal. His relationships with his wife and Junior are frequently placed on the back burner as phone calls from distressed customers disturb family dinners and business demands keep him away from home and from Little League games. The family's social life revolves around the business.

1961 Fifteen-year-old Junior is being significantly affected by his identification with the family business. The business's visibility in the community subjects him to peer judgments by friends and schoolmates. He's starting to think about his career, and whether the family business is for him. The dinner table, which Dad can now afford to frequent more often, is abuzz with conversation about the business and its problems.

1966 The business is thriving and Dad, at forty-five, is in the prime of his life. The business is being competently run, giving him time to lend his visibility to a community cause or two and to be active in the Chamber of Commerce and the Rotary Club. Junior, meanwhile, is having a ball at college. He spends school vacations earning spending money driving a delivery truck or running errands and doing office work for the business. He and Dad have the occasional "serious" heart-to-heart about his future—and whether it involves the family business.

1971 Dad's golden years loom on the horizon. At fifty, he's in his stride, but this awareness infiltrates his planning. Some of his friends die suddenly, prompting him to see an estate planner and actually start to use the physical fitness facilities at the club. He toys with slowing down . . . but is soon back up to speed. He looks at Junior's bright future and sees *his* past. His eagerness to see the business continue beyond him, and to pass it on successfully to Junior, competes with fear of giving up control and becoming "George who?" Retirement planning must begin, as must training for Junior, who meanwhile has spent most of his time in the company in the sales department—why? Because that's where Dad got his start. Now, though, Dad begins to consider industry training programs and other education for Junior. The term "the boss's kid" and the resentment by some of the salespeople of him is beginning to grate on Junior's nerves. He is hurt to find that some employees have used his friendship to make points with the boss. Sometimes he resents Dad for placing him in this position. He wonders if he could make it on his own. Dad's authority seems overwhelming. It permeates every corner of the business; he's the business symbol in every television, radio, and newspaper ad. This power is felt by each member of the business, especially by Junior.

1976 Junior's confidence has been enhanced by the last five years of training and some small successes with his own projects for the business. He's also had a couple of screw-ups—some pretty serious. It's vital at this stage that Dad let him take his lumps. This won't be easy for Dad—his take-charge personality won't want to allow it—but experience is the only teacher. Dad is also struggling, of course, with memories of picking Junior up after he fell out of the tree when he was little and comforting him as he sobbed in his arms. Sometimes Dad asks Junior to "look after things" while he's away. This conveys the successorship message to the other employees that Junior is their future boss.

1981 This can be the most dangerous period for the successorship process. Dad, at sixty, is slowing down and becoming more conservative, while thirty-five-year-old Junior is raring to go ahead with new ideas and changes. When he proposes new ventures, though, Dad unintentionally resists, forgetting that his son is displaying the same ambition he did at that age. Dad is more concerned with setting up retirement income and planning his estate. His consideration of new ventures include a newly added factor—limited time. Junior brings his frustration home to his wife and two children, and his wife's opinions are added to the pot. Trying to please both his father and his wife sometimes tears him apart. It is vital at this stage that Dad and Junior be clear with each other about Junior's authority and responsibility in the business and about the upcoming transfer of power.

1986 If Dad hasn't started to make succession plans concrete by setting up stock transfers, buyout agreements, franchise arrangements, or the like, forty-year-old Junior may begin to lose interest in the business. Several of his friends may have successful businesses, while he is in second place as (still) the boss's son. He begins to wonder if he made the right decision, but is deterred from leaving by loyalty to the very person who is frustrating him. Dad, meanwhile, is absorbed with panicky thoughts of retirement. If he can put these aside and coach Junior to take over the business and not simply treat him as heir-apparent, their relationship and the business will survive this stressful time.

1987 Dad's unexpected death creates turmoil as Junior is thrust into leadership without experience in areas that were previously his father's private domain. Although he's had some preparation, a great deal of luck will be necessary for the business to survive this sudden removal of its long-time leader and caretaker.

As our fictional but possible family history shows, planning for the transfer of power is not a simple process that can be undertaken a couple of years before the owner's retirement. At each stage of the parent/owner's and the successor's lives, different issues must be addressed, different emotions acknowledged. This means that the owner must accept his mortality early on and plan for this transfer for it to be successful. Developing a succession plan does not necessarily mean that the parent/owner promptly gives up complete control of the business. This may not happen for several years. The point is that the parent/owner must make a declaration that the process is under way, ultimately resulting in his stepping aside for the next generation.

During a recent successorship workshop, one of the participants, an active and alert octogenarian, shared a problem he was having with his son, who was in the business with him. It seems that this sixty-year-old successor has notified his father that he plans to retire from the business at the end of the year!

Remember, it's crucial to share your future plans with your successor and keep your successorship agreement.

Nurturing Enthusiasm and Confidence

A family who owns a prominent business in the community is treated as something of a novelty by the local people. It seems that every encounter turns into a conversation about an experience that person had with one of your employees. Well, your children receive the same treatment in the community and at school, and they didn't ask for it.

Children of the owner of a family business grow up in the public eye, to a degree, and their privacy is hampered. This is a classic two-edged sword: Some children grow up feeling like celebrities, and become eager to join the business, while others tire of the constant association by the time they reach adulthood.

Nat Shulman remembers his daughter's request for a used Volkswagen when she got her driver's license. She had taken driver's education in Chevrolet automobiles loaned to her high school by his dealership. Although she was proud of the family business's reputation in town, she said she was "becoming OD'd on Best Chevy's influence" on her life. Hence the request for an anonymous and ordinary car.

As Shulman remembers: "My reaction was explosive. I told her that as long as Chevrolet was the principal financial support of the family, she would drive a Chevy. If she wanted to drive 'that foreign car,' she could go live with a Volkswagen family! Also, didn't she realize that by driving around town in her Chevy she would influence her friends and their families to buy cars from us? She ended up with a four-year-old Chevy.

"As I look back over twenty-five years during which our family coexisted with our business in the community, I see how often the interests of the family were influenced by the needs of the business. I viewed most family members' activities during this period according to how they would affect the community's image of the business.

"At least I can take heart from the knowledge that I'm far from alone in this area. During my research over the last fifteen years, I have observed fellow members of local Chambers of Commerce, Rotary Clubs, Kiwanis, etc. In most cases, the impact of the business on the family was similar to mine. In some cases, the impact of the community on the family and the business was harsh enough to irreparably damage the family."

As head of The Center for Entrepreneurial Management, Inc. and its Chief Executive Officers Club, nonprofit organizations he founded to help entrepreneurs, Joe Mancuso probably knows more entrepreneurs than anyone else. According to Mancuso, some 40 percent of all CEO Club members claim they are family businesses, yet academic institutions and MBA curricula have failed to differentiate this segment of business from non-family-run businesses. As a result, he hears distressing family business stories from CEO Club members all the time.

The Thomas Warren Realty Company was a successful development and real estate company in New England. Tom Warren and his wife had two sons and a daughter. He was an innovative realtor who would buy houses and often literally move them from one location to a more desirable one, thereby increasing their value.

Warren Realty "For Sale" signs were the most prominent real estate signs in town, dramatically increasing the family's visibility. Compounding this sensitive status, Tom often had to personally appear before town zoning boards and meetings to request zoning changes. He was an ethical developer who contributed greatly toward responsibly expanding the real estate tax base; however, any zoning change affects many voters.

Those discontented town residents had a dramatic effect on the family's life in the town. The three kids were constantly reminded by friends of the Warren family's impact on the town's profile. The children saw their father being castigated by townspeople jealous of his success. They watched as he was denied ordinary town cooperation in mutually beneficial projects, because his name was Warren. These scenarios squelched the kids' desire to succeed their father in the family business. The family and the business suffered.

There are many successful family business/community relationships through which the lives of family members have been enriched, but don't expect to be guaranteed a smooth ride for you or your children. Remember that how the kids feel about the business as they grow up will determine their eagerness to participate as adults. If they are feeling confined by the association, don't push it.

Any son or daughter who does survive high school with enthusiasm for the family business intact might be interested in an industry training program. The retail automobile industry is really ahead of the game here.

In 1961, the National Automobile Dealers Association (NADA) met with Northwood Institute, which has campuses in Michigan, Florida, and Texas, to develop a dynamic learning center for youths interested in careers in the retail auto industry. This effort culminated in 1973 with the dedication of the NADA Automotive Marketing Center on Northwood's Michigan campus. This center was built with funds raised entirely by the automobile dealers of America and is a tribute to the men and women of vision who realized the need to heighten the professional status of their field.

Another unique and comprehensive training resource for aspiring new-car dealers is the NADA Dealer Candidate Academy, which currently offers six concurrent, twelve-month classes with twenty candidates. Seventy-five percent of the Academy's graduates are currently successful owners or managers of new-car and new-truck franchises across the country.

A big part of the curriculum is hands-on training under the department heads of the dealership in the daily work of the candidates. This really helps establish the relationships between the candidate and the very people he may one day manage. This course also covers estate planning, successorship buy-sell agreements, and legal liabilities and responsibilities. You might consider working toward having your own industry association start one. An extensive NADA survey found that most dealers did expect their progeny to succeed them, but felt uncomfortable about training them. Similarly, most sons and daughters participating in NADA workshops agreed that a solid training program allowing them to be judged individually and to develop some skills away from the family was necessary.

Another useful program is CEO's Family Business Experience Program, three days of intensive seminars for the entire family at Big Rock Valley Farm in Cassopolis, Michigan. The program's success comes from its combination of education with "enforced togetherness" that family business members are usually too busy to ever experience.

No matter how good the training program, though, it can't give your son or daughter one crucial thing: experience. Let's say you've done everything right—as they were growing up, you tried not to impose the business on their personal life and you've managed to protect their natural interest and enthusiasm for the family business. You sent them to a good training program and now they're ready to jump in with both feet.

Well, here comes the hardest part: letting them screw up. Many next-generation family members enter the family business with limited knowledge and experience with economic downturns in the marketplace, for example. There are no words available to prepare a neophyte manager to deal with a recession and depressed market. In this area, experience is not only the best teacher . . . it's the only teacher!

The retail auto dealers who survived the monumental shakeout that occurred during the late seventies when OPEC flexed its muscle and many consumers turned away from American cars experienced a boom in sales and profits from 1983 into 1988. Early during these boom years, Shulman transferred management control of his company to his son, Scott, who had shown a lot of gumption during the aforementioned shakeout. He became a superstar within the industry during this period—sales and profits had never been better—and he began to consider expanding to other locations.

Meanwhile, overhead expenses had risen dramatically and layers of bureaucracy had materialized, going unnoticed because of the sales and profit boom. Scott had negotiated for another franchise in a different state and Nat was frankly relieved when the purchase didn't go through. He saw his son spreading his management abilities too thin. Nat was too intimidated by his own lack of involvement in the day-to-day operation of the business and the burgeoning sales figures to say much. He had an uneasy feeling, though, that when the marketplace began its leveling off, the lack of attention to good basic business practices, particularly to a strong service operation, would seriously hurt the company.

Lo and behold, a chain of negative circumstances began in July 1988, beginning with a serious injury to the comptroller and a major in-house computer screw-up. New car and truck sales began to soften. Scott, meanwhile, was busily negotiating for an additional dealership in a neighboring town.

Negotiations for the new dealership continued for more than three months, during which the daily operational threats taking place were ignored. The attitude in the dealership about the ominous signals coming from the marketplace was that "this is just a hiccup in the market."

The three banks considering financing the new dealership had all been told beforehand that Nat would not be involved in the deal and had given no indication that this would affect their decision. Ultimately, though, all three banks demanded that he endorse or guarantee the loans. This was unacceptable to Scott and Nat. As Scott put it, "You're not going to have to put your life's work on the line for this deal!" So the new venture became a nonevent.

Coincident with this downturn, Scott was distracted from the task at hand by some personal financial problems with a piece of speculative real estate.

Nat had made a firm resolution not to become involved in the day-to-day operation of the business unless he was asked to help or an emergency developed. It was difficult, but necessary for Scott's growth. So he stayed away, closely observing, however, the expense-saving steps being taken to compensate for the loss in business. His opinion was that this is the way lifelong lessons are learned by successor candidates.

After heavy losses during the first quarter of 1989, Nat returned to the business to find a frightened, shaken young entrepreneur experiencing a severe trial by fire that threatened his whole business career. Scott's confidence was severely damaged and he was upset about being forced to cut 30 percent of the management and employees. He asked for his father's help and support. After a few months they got back on track, though the damage to Scott's self-confidence took longer to heal.

Nat's first task was to reassure him that he "hadn't lost his fastball," while not letting him ignore the fact that he had been seduced by a bonanza market into poor management habits that cost him dearly in the ensuing downturn. Also, Nat reminded Scott that the disappointment of letting Nat down was less important than the business losses, which had cut deeply into his own inheritance.

We've already discussed the hazards of being fair, but at a time like this, it's important to be emotionally fair. In other words, it's *not* fair to stand by and let your son or daughter take the lumps and then waltz in with "I told you so's" and other traditional parental observations. Simply acknowledge that it sometimes rains on everyone's parade, and take the necessary objective steps to weather the storm. Believe us, they're suffering enough!

On the other hand, it is unwise to keep stepping in to save the day before any damage is done, because the lessons learned may be invaluable. Assess the potential impact and if it's not too great, let it happen! The lesson learned may be the bargain of the century. Better that it be learned while you're still around.

It's not uncommon for the children of a successful business owner to become turned off to the business before they even get to the "tough lessons" phase. Sometimes they fall victim to the family's growing affluence, such as the great hotelier Conrad Hilton's son Nicky. Nicky came home one day with an expensive pair of shoes. His father protested, "I've never paid that much for a pair of shoes in my life." To which Nicky replied, "Ah! But you never had a rich father." And if Conrad had had a rich father, would he have had the drive to build his chain of hotels? The success of the first generation can breed the complacency of the second.

Furthermore, it's not unusual for a father to inadvertently poison the business for the children. Leon Danco, founder and president of the Cleveland-based Center for Family Business, describes a typical scenario: "Dad comes home and over dinner tells the kids how the competitors are no damn good, the suppliers won't deliver, the customers won't pay, and how the government is taking what little he has left. Then Dad puts his arm around his kid and says, 'And someday, Son, this will all be yours.' "

What Dad usually neglects to say is that he loves the business, that the kids could too, and that all the aggravation is just part of being successful. This love for the business is what he must pass on to his children if it is to survive. With that in mind, here are three suggestions for perpetuating growth, confidence, and entrepreneurship in a family-owned business:

1. Develop an organizational chart for the business. Let people know where they stand. This is crucial both for family members and outside managers. This helps prevent "fairness"—when you're having a difficult time promoting one child over another, even when merit demands the promotion, for example. For management to be effective, the structure has to be stable and unwaffling.
2. Let the kids make mistakes. A powerful parent often dominates the business and the family until the children are reluctant to compete. The problem is compounded when what little authority they may have gained is snatched back after a minor mistake or two.
3. Establish clear and consistent boundaries between business issues and emotional issues within the family. Keep issues about the home at home and issues about the business at the office. Lines must be drawn and agreed upon before a problem occurs, or valuable time and energy will be taken away from the business when you need it most.

DON'T PLAY "DYNASTY"

It is not written in the stars or anywhere else in the universe that an owner's relative qualifies for or will want control of the family business because he or she is a blood relation! As we discussed above, enthusiasm for the family business can be a precarious thing, and yet there may be an attitude among the owner's sons and daughters that they have an inalienable right to the family's legacy, and they don't have to make much of a commitment to receive it.

Let's make it clear: The law of the land supports the theory that a relative has a right to estate assets, if there was no specified wish from the deceased. The choice of chief operating officer, however, *lies solely with the family members who have inherited the stock and assets of the business*.

We've already discussed the perils of "fairness." Usually, not only does the senior generation want to treat each member of the younger generation fairly, but it often wants the chief operating officer to come from that generation. Simply because Isadore Goldberg was an expert in manufacturing women's dresses, however, doesn't mean that his son Joshua or his daughter Rebecca care two figs about the Goldberg Dress Company beyond their warm feelings for the benefits they may receive. They may abhor the dress industry! Why, then, must the senior generation insist that these unwilling successor candidates be part of the search for a new head of the business?

Many times, a surviving family's interest is best served if:

- The heirs promote a nonfamily CEO from within the company and distribute income-producing stock among the passive stockholders.
- An eligible nonfamily top management person is allowed to buy a minority interest in the business and to establish a long-term buyout up to an agreed-upon percentage. With this arrangement, the family maintains control, avoids undesirable investors, and allows the buyout to come only from future bonuses and profits of the business.
- An objective, competent, paid board of directors from outside the family is established to meet quarterly and advise on the progress of operating plans and budgets.
- The business is sold at peak value, in the most tax-advantageous way, and a inite trust is created for family members. This ensures the security of family members who aren't interested in continuing the family's operation of the business.
- The image of the business as a dynasty is replaced with a pragmatic

assessment of what will best serve the long-term interests of the family and the business.

Keep in mind that family members need not go into the family business. If there are no excellent successor candidates in the family, consider selling the business! Don't force it.

Again, being fair with family members is fine when dealing with real estate, stock and bond portfolios, and other assets of the family business, but it is an extremely dangerous and inappropriate way to deal with the power and control of the business. Also, don't push unfit or uninterested sons and daughters into key management positions simply because competent siblings are in similar positions.

Share the Dream

Why are family business owners reluctant to share their dreams of the future with their heirs? Is it because they fear that by sharing their plan for their estate and business they will hurry its implementation? Is it because the future will go away if we don't talk about it? Do years of keeping closemouthed about sensitive business information breed a lack of trust in sharing confidential information with family members? An owner may feel, for example, that his successor's spouse cannot be trusted with this kind of knowledge, or may fear that the spouse could use such information during a divorce. Finally, the head of the business may worry that commitments to successor candidates are irrevocable.

Within the family business, dedicated and talented successor candidates are often kept in the dark by caring owner/parents, not just about pertinent business information but about their job futures. In some cases the child is hampered by his or her love and respect for a parent/owner from criticizing flawed policies in the company. It is difficult for a son or daughter to suddenly shift gears when the revered parent also becomes his or her boss. Many parent/owners innocently and sometimes cruelly exploit this love and respect.

Spouses of successors can become very frustrated when they encounter this exploitation and are powerless to challenge it. Spouses are often able to view family relationships more objectively, simply because they can evaluate the participants without years of old family baggage. It's not a mystery to understand why the successor is often caught in a tug-of-war between his spouse and the owner that causes damage not only to the business but to the marriage as well. And such irreparable damage is all done in the name of love. In the name of love, too, spouses ignore the protection of pre- and postnuptial agreements, convinced by their current feelings that such agreements will never be necessary. Woe to the spouse who, out of love, hesitates to ask for an upgrade of the nuptial agreements when the other party's income jumps. Just look at Ivana Trump, being asked to settle for a paltry $25 million of the Donald's billion-dollar fortune, a fortune she (by many accounts) worked almost as hard for as he did. Her failure to periodically upgrade their agreement to keep it in line with their wealth could cost her dearly in their divorce.

Jerry Green was forty-two years old and had a lovely wife and three handsome young boys aged eight, ten and fourteen. He had worked in his seventy-eight-year-old father's business for the past twenty years. His sister had recently married an aggressive attorney who was pushing her to research her potential stake in the family business. Jerry was the only family member who had actively participated in the business—in fact, his father had spent most of his time as a career politician and for several years Jerry ran the business himself.

When we interviewed this fine young couple, we asked them about the family's plans for Jerry to take over the total management and ownership of the business from his father. They replied that they had never been told of any plans but were "sure there was something." They were reluctant to raise the issue at this time because his father had cancer.

It was heart-rending to see the pain in Jerry's eyes as he spoke of his father's illness, but we wanted to shout: "What about your lovely wife and three fine sons in the picture you so proudly showed me? What's their reward for sharing you with the business for the last twenty years? It's too bad your dad's got cancer and you love him so much, but what will happen when he dies? You and your family have a right to know what your future holds!"

Jerry finally said that he had questioned his father about a successorship plan, only to have his father beg off each time with the excuse that he didn't have time to talk about it.

We have talked with dozens of mature, talented successor candidates who have spent years working with parent/owners and never developed buy–sell agreements or any other plans for their prospective ownership of the family business. Many of them offer the same reason for this ignorance as Jerry did: "Dad was too busy to talk about it when I asked him."

Interviews with attorneys have revealed the paranoia that many of their clients display over relinquishing control when constructing estate plans and wills. Clients attempt to control their heirs' fortunes from the grave by placing all kinds of complicated conditions on the disbursement of funds and assets.

One client, who died twenty-two years ago, was obsessed with saving as much of the estate taxes as was legally possible, even to the detriment of his heirs. In order to save the maximum, he left the entire estate to his wife, who in turn would leave the future taxable estate to the two sons when she died. Delaying the inheritance tax until his wife died would allow his money to keep working "for the family's benefit" during her lifetime, he reasoned. A minimal amount of money was disbursed to the two sons at the time of his death, with the provision that they could ask their mother for help in case of dire need.

The mother lived to the ripe old age of ninety-seven and died in a nursing home. She was severely incapacitated and seldom recognized her sons when they came to visit during her last five years.

By the time the two sons received their inheritance, they were in their seventies. Each had had serious heart bypass operations and were not expected to equal their mother's longevity. So the father's obsession with saving taxes twenty-two years ago will ultimately deposit his money with grandchildren he didn't even know. If that's how you want your money spent, that's OK, but if it isn't, you'd better start planning how you will turn over the business during your lifetime.

Modern successful business organizations operate in an environment of open and free communication between top management and their personnel. Why should family businesses be any different?

New management styles invite participation in operating decisions from production line workers, and reports to stockholders by major corporations are filled with all sorts of sales and profit information. The incomes of top management teams are reported in the public press.

Top-level managers in modern businesses are generally well informed about the parameters of their jobs. Many work under contracts that explicitly define their relationships with their companies and their options to purchase stock, usually at favorable prices. Again, why should the family business environment be any more cloistered?

There are no rules that will adequately cover all the communication problems between parents and children in business together, but here are a few basic suggestions:

Mom and Dad:

- Keep your estate plan as simple as possible, and don't try to control your heirs' lives from the grave.
- Tell your successors what will happen financially to them when you die.
- Don't ignore your children's requests for information about their future in the business.
- Instead of looking at your sons and daughters through the eyes of loving parents, try to perceive them with the eyes of a business owner looking to

ensure the perpetuity of a life's work through a capable custodian. Would this custodian be satisfied with having no information about the future?

- Allow your fledgling entrepreneurs to make mistakes—this is the cheapest education in the school of hard knocks.

Sons and Daughters:

- Don't accept "I haven't got time to talk right now" more than half a dozen times. Get in the car together for a long drive away from protective distractions like telephones, lock the doors, and talk! One person talks on the way out, the other talks on the way back. Mancuso knows a widow who runs a dress shop who takes walks with her son when there is some conflict that needs discussing. She talks on the way to their destination, and he gives his opinions on the way home.
- If the communication problem persists, seek professional help or ask a family friend or valued business associate to intervene.
- Don't ignore input from your spouse. He or she often sees the proverbial trees in the family forest more clearly than you do.
- Finally, don't neglect to share experiences outside the business. Go to the health club together or to a sports activity or show. Take in industry functions such as seminars and workshops together.

Remember the fundamental problem in family business relationships: The dynamics that best serve a family are not necessarily beneficial to a business. To keep both your family and your business strife-free, you must recognize these different dynamics and address them intelligently and honestly. Love alone won't cut it in both arenas!

The Withdrawal Period

Odd things happen to people when money, power, and control become part of their daily existence. Nat and his son shared more than twenty great, intimate years prior to his son's entry into the business, yet a few years after the son assumed a management position in the business, a power struggle between them developed. In retrospect, Nat can see that, because of his son's tremendous motivation to succeed without "Dad's" influence, he felt threatened by Nat's presence in the business. Their close relationship actually exacerbated the problem, as it was difficult for Scott, the busy CEO, to respond to Nat's reluctance to let go of daily involvement in the operation of the business.

They started with small things, like the morning mail. Each business morning for twenty-five years, the morning mail was delivered to Nat's desk to be opened by him personally and passed on to the office manager for distribution. Personally opening the business mail enabled Nat to open a window into the inner workings of the organization. Customer complaint letters that otherwise might have been ignored received his immediate attention and follow-up. New purchasing trends by department heads were apparent, as were any insidious expense abuses.

Nat enthusiastically instructed his son/successor, "Personally open the dealership mail, whenever possible!" Of course, he had intended for Scott to heed this suggestion sometime in the future, perhaps while Nat was vacationing in Hawaii for the winter. Scott thought the suggestion was so good that since the day Nat told him about it, he personally started opening the mail. There were mornings (Nat's ashamed to say) when Nat sat at his office window watching for the mail truck, raced out to greet the mailman, grabbed the bundle of mail, and retreated to his office like a predator with its prey, before his son could get to it.

They have since agreed that it is more important for the son to handle the morning mail, but several similar situations occurred before Nat ultimately learned to let go. Similar incidents are assuredly taking place in most family businesses throughout the United States.

At times, Nat felt rejected during the withdrawal period, and he reacted with some power-and-control moves undoubtedly also used by most business owners in America, such as making a big fuss over cigarette butts in showroom entrances, or insisting that all new cars on display in the yard have their front wheels straight. Sounds ridiculous, doesn't it?

For Nat and his son, an outside consulting firm was even required at one point to resolve their power-and-control battle—but more about that in chapter 5. The most noteworthy event during the entire transition process was the disappearance of the son's defensive attitude toward Nat's intrusions. As his level of confidence in running the company increased, his defensive posture toward his father decreased almost in direct proportion. This ratio is at the core of many acts of unkindness and rejection by the players in the successorship process. The old cliché "it takes two to tango" was never more appropriate. The lack of confidence of the new generation combines with the anxiety of the owner at the prospect of retirement to create nasty scenes.

Don't carry around this resentment like an undigested meal in your gut. Talk about it. Fight about it, but in private. Share your real feelings about untenable management arrangements with each other, away from ears that would privately enjoy the prospect of the successor's failure. Don't accept cop-outs like "I don't have time to talk about it right now." The response to that statement is:

"When?" Finally, negotiate a plan for transition that will serve the daily needs of all active family business members, not just the ones who wield the power and control.

It seems logical that there should be no conflicts if a parent/owner is willing to turn the business over to a son or daughter who is qualified and serious about the responsibility. Unfortunately, we're not dealing with logic here, but with emotions. According to Aristotle, logic only works on small decisions. The big ones all involve emotion.

The owner is still anxious about leaving a lifetime routine. The successor is eager to take over and is impatient with the owner's inability to let go. Both the parent/owner and the succeeding son or daughter should recognize the other's shortcomings and offer understanding and encouragement. Treat each other with dignity and respect, as any business partners would treat each other if they weren't related. And expect each other's emotional needs to change constantly. After all, as an old Greek proverb says: You can't step over the same stream twice. Even if you walk over it on the same rocks, the stream, everflowing, is always different.

THREE'S A CROWD

Even if a succession has been planned carefully, and the withdrawal phase has been survived, there can still be problems. One of Joe Mancuso's consulting assignments will illustrate this point. In the early 1900s, two brothers started a small paint company in Quincy, Massachusetts. The company survived the Depression and provided a good living for their families. Both brothers married and had children. One had a son, the other had two sons, and eventually all three boys joined the family business—here was the core of the families' business problem.

When the two brothers retired, they left their sons in control, and what had been a 50–50 ownership became 50–25–25. This setup created a tendency for one of the two brothers to vote with a cousin to avoid conflict. The temptation in such an arrangement becomes for attention and energy to be devoted to the relationships between the owners, and away from the business.

You've heard the old saw that three's a crowd. Well, it's just as true in family business. Working as a consultant on this problem, Joe devised a rotating scheme in which each of the three sons took a nine-month sabbatical while the other two managed the business. The first brother left for nine months, while the second brother and the cousin ran the business. Then brother number two took a fully paid sabbatical. Then the cousin. Every combination of two had a chance to work together over an eighteen-month period. The process produced harmony in the business and gave each of the managers an opportunity to understand the other relative's function. Instead of the business being sold off and all going away mad, as had been threatened, each of the two brothers decided he'd be happier running his own company. The cousin was happy to buy them out. The original company survived intact, two new companies were formed, and nobody came away with hard feelings.

This story illustrates a common occurrence in family businesses that are passed down from parent to children: the dilution of ownership. As the stock becomes more dispersed, those most concerned with running the business lose more control. In turn, the stockholders, often no longer simply two or three close families, get upset about how the company is being managed and try to force a sellout to a third party. It may be best for key members of the family to continually prune the stock structure by buying out family members who aren't active participants in the business.*

* Today the issues of parenting are much more complex. The definition of family is changing more rapidly than the field of business. Children can be born via in-vitro fertilization, and the old title of Mommy and Daddy now depends. Is it the biological mother, or the mother who carried the embryo for nine months? They are not always the same person. Then the "real" Mommy could be neither of these two choices, but the woman who raised the child.

Joe Mancuso has a three-year-old son, Max, and a two-year-old granddaughter, Jaeda, and they play together. Max was calling Joe Daddy, but baby Jaeda calls him Grandpa Joe. After the two children were together for a while, Max kept searching the room for "Grandpa Joe." After all was explained to him, he elected to call Joe "Grandpa Daddy." If you think the issues presented here are complex, just wait twenty-five years when Max and Jaeda are both old enough to read this book and want to work in the "family business." It's not going to get easier to solve these issues as they get more complex.

3. The Ins and Outs of In-Laws

THE FIRST STEP TOWARD A WORKING RELATIONSHIP THAT WORKS: UNDERSTANDING YOUR SON- OR DAUGHTER-IN-LAW'S FEARS

Although a family business owner may have a solid idea of who will succeed as CEO upon his or her retirement, this picture can change when in-laws enter the family. Many times, the new son- or daughter-in-law is a strong contender for a top management position. Often, when an in-law is being considered for a job in the family business, little heed is paid to his or her identity needs and potential feelings of second-class citizenship. It is the rare owner who appreciates how hard it will be for an in-law to feel fulfilled by a career in the family business. Many times, in-law parent/owners adopt the attitude of benefactors, as though they have granted the in-law a tremendous gift unattainable anywhere else.

On the plus side, an in-law comes into the family business free of the emotional baggage that clouds the objectivity of those who grew up together. The brother-in-law never saw his brother-in-law as a helpless infant, or his mother-in-law as a loving, protective parent. He may be a step ahead of the family's own children in becoming an effective, unbiased manager. Sons- and daughters-in-law are relieved of the overprotection that owners inflict on adult sons and daughters. Parents carry mental pictures of their children—how they looked on their first day of school, what it was like to comfort them when they fell playing, having to constantly remind them not to talk to strangers or play with matches. In many family businesses, parent/owners try too hard to protect their successor candidates from failure and pain, simply because this protection is what the parent is accustomed to providing. They fail to see that denying successors the right to make mistakes and suffer the results retards their growth. In this regard, in-law children have a distinct advantage.

Conversely, a son- or daughter-in-law can serve as a lightning rod for family hostility. Sons-in-law sometimes initially accept a position in their wife's family's business to assure that his wife will be kept in the manner to which she is accustomed. Even if such a son-in-law turns out to be a bright young man with much potential, his job security may be based on the quality of his family life. Any problems, and he may become "that werewolf in bed with my little girl" to the boss, vulnerable to the venting of all of a father's classic overprotective tendencies. A son-in-law assigned the position coveted by the owner's son may face a lot of resentment. Or, he may wonder if a top position was offered only because he married the boss's daughter, regardless of his own merit. And what if he doesn't want the position? Will his father-in-law be offended? What if the in-law spends many years in the business, but eventually divorces the boss's kid? Will he lose his job?

In addition to those mentioned above, here are some typical concerns floating through the mind of an in-law about to take a position in the spouse's family business:

- Would I be offered this salary if I weren't married to the boss's child?
- How will it affect my marriage if I turn down the offer? If I do go into the business, what will happen to my personal life?
- Will I be sorry that I never pursued the careers I was considering before this? Could I be equally successful on my own?
- How well do I get along with my spouse's brothers and sisters? Will they resent me?
- Will this force my spouse to always feel torn between me and the rest of the family?
- Shouldn't I assume that the boss's primary goal will be the welfare of my spouse and our children? Won't my welfare be secondary?
- Would my spouse respect me more if I stayed out of the business?
- On the other hand, don't I owe it to my spouse and children to accept this opportunity?
- How will my position be perceived by business associates, staff, and friends? Will my spouse start to feel as if I got married just for the business opportunities? How much will I be bothered by those kinds of suspicions?
- Will my spouse always be the conduit through which I will receive a percentage of ownership in the firm?

- What sort of problems will arrive when my kids are old enough to work in the business? Will they face competition and hostility from cousins and uncles?

The validity of these concerns doesn't matter. The point is that owners and their families need to be sensitive to the position of a son- or daughter-in-law placed in the family business.

When writing a book like this one, it's almost impossible to avoid sounding preachy! And no one, especially CEOs and entrepreneurs, likes to be told what to do—just read our comments in appendix I about the traits of these unusual people. If you tell them what to do, you automatically encourage them to do just the opposite.

In a family business, the tendency is for family members to judge each other by intentions and to judge everyone else by their actions. As in sports, intentions in a family business aren't enough, no matter how good they are. Let's use prizefighting as an example since it is easily the oldest and cruelest individual sport. It's a rough, tough business where good intentions are rare and are rarely good enough.

A father is seldom, if ever, a good manager/coach for a son. Jerry Quarry, a heavyweight, and Howard Davis, an Olympic gold medal winner as a lightweight, are just two of the boxers who were managed by their fathers and who may have, consequently, failed to reach their full potential. Buster Douglas, the heavyweight champ who knocked out Mike Tyson, was formerly managed by his dad (also a pretty good fighter), but reached new heights after he switched to a new manager. The lesson is that it's almost impossible to fully mature when you have the same mentor as a child and as an adult. A father who stays too long as a mentor is depriving the child of new perspectives.

Parent/mentors who don't see this in their own family usually are blinded by love. It's a crime how much evil is done in family business in the name of love. Remember, a good leader causes people to have confidence in the leader, but a great leader causes people to have confidence in themselves.

As we mentioned, it may be an advantage for a successor candidate or top manager not to have had a long history with the family. In many family businesses, parent/owners try too hard to protect their children from failure and pain, simply because this is what their job has always been as parents. They have a hard time seeing that making mistakes and experiencing pain are catalysts for knowledge and experience, and that denying successors this right retards their growth.

Sons- and daughters-in-law, on the other hand, come into the business as adults and are perceived as such. No lifelong agenda distorts the picture. Neither do they sport the feeling of entitlement that can stunt the growth of blood successors who have spent their entire lives under the umbrella of the family business. This feeling of entitlement—that the business is "owed" to them—can often severely debilitate their efforts in the business. The in-law, on the other hand, has reason to feel compelled to put out 110 percent in order to be accepted and gain respect.

There even may be better communication between the owner and a son- or daughter-in-law, simply because the significantly lessened degree of emotional attachment may allow for more objective and candid dialogue about business matters.

The Stickiest Issue: Stock Equity

The gulf between blood siblings and in-laws is most apparent when it comes time to allocate stock in the company, either upon the demise or retirement of the owner, or in the normal course of business. The real question underlying stock allocation, of course, is: Who is going to own and control the business? This kind of question seems to bring out the vulture in us all.

There have been cases of collusion between fathers and daughters in which the son-in-law was used to provide material security for "Daddy's little girl" and her children. In these cases, total equity positions were arranged so that they were controlled by the daughter/wife forever, that is, as long as the couple stayed married, the husband had a good job, or other stipulations. Conversely, Joe tells the story of a Harvard Business School classmate who threatened that his father-in-law would never see the grandchildren again unless he was named president of the company.

There is something regressive and unfair about the owner of a business arranging his affairs so that his CEO must remain the husband of his daughter in order to maintain his position in the company! Many nonconstricting stock equity plans can be tailored by competent tax attorneys and accountants to accomplish any goal of future ownership of the company the parent/owner desires without placing immovable obstacles in the growth path of talented in-laws.

Perhaps a person small on talent and drive would tolerate the prospect of being dependent on his or her spouse for career rewards, but a highly motivated, talented, committed individual deserves some form of equity reward that clearly and simply provides him or her with respect—not just as an appendage of the family. If your son-in-law is doing a great job, make the same efforts to keep him around that you would for any valuable top manager, regardless of the status of the marriage. Division of stock among family members, including in-laws, during the owner's lifetime can be an exhilarating and powerful experience, not to mention a good tax move. Businesses in which one individual holds most or all of the stock are usually rife with power and control battles. Parent/owners must honestly consider worthy in-laws in their successorship planning and avoid playing the "as long as you're good to our little girl (or boy) you've got a place in the family business" game.

A good example of doing it right is the Imagineering Company in South Bend, Indiana, controlled by the father, David Huber. Dave is the chairman, but the president is James Hammer, a talented executive who happens to be married to Dave's oldest child. Working for Jim are both Dave's son and daughter as well as another brother-in-law, married to Dave's second daughter. To say Jim Hammer is between a rock and a hard place is simply inadequate. Let's restate his role in other words, or in his view: (1) He reports to his father-in-law. (2) He supervises his two brothers-in-law and a sister-in-law. When this family attended a three-day CEO Club Family Business Experience program, Jim's peers were shocked that he was succeeding in his role. So when you're having problems with one or more family business members, remember, if Jim did it, so can you.

The Daughter-in-Law as Successor

While we're on the subject of worthy successors, don't overlook your daughter-in-law. We learned of a case several years ago that demonstrates there are no rules in successorship, only circumstances.

J. B. owned an electrical supply company in partnership (65 percent/35 percent) with his thirty-seven-year-old son, an only child. Steven was happily married to Claudia and had three young children, when he was stricken with terminal cancer. The business had purchased life insurance on each of the partners, so it would have been simple for J. B. to just hand over the sizable proceeds from the policy to Claudia—which, coupled with J. B.'s potential inheritance, would provide economic security for her and the children for many years.

Claudia had a better idea, however. She was thirty-five, healthy, and ambitious, with a degree in Business Administration, and all three kids were in school for the workday. During the years she was married to Steven, there was always a lot of talk about the business in their home, and he had valued her opinions and feedback. She proposed to J. B. that she come into the business to be trained as a successor candidate by J. B., who was sixty-five, and by her husband for as long as he could physically manage it.

Claudia and J. B. agreed that if she ever remarried after Steven died, the value of her stock at the time of his death would go into trust for the three children. All she would realize from that time forward was the appreciation on her share of her stock in the company plus whatever Steven would will exclusively to her. Wasn't that a clever arrangement? We call it "win-win."

J. B. agreed to the idea, recognizing it could continue the business beyond his lifetime. Within three years, he retired and currently two of his grandsons are working in the family business. This wonderful story would not have happened had Claudia not grabbed for the brass ring. Who is to say that two of her great-granddaughters might not be the next "family" to control this business?

THE SHORTCHANGING OF IN-LAWS

The shortchanging of in-laws is a common but misguided practice in many family businesses in the United States. Talented in-laws receive minimal consideration for successor positions. Often, their equity positions are based more on their performance as spouse or parent than on job performance. When stock is distributed to an in-law, it is usually with conditions that severely restrict the sale or transfer of it, especially if the marriage should fail. Consider whether this is a motivator or a demotivator.

Many times parent/owners have publicly extolled the value and commitment of sons- or daughters-in-law, even stating the in-law was easier to work with than the blood children. Yet, when the time comes to distribute or will stock in the company, the same owners have been reluctant to adequately compensate the hardworking in-law.

In his book, *Inside the Family-Held Business*, Milton Stern writes, "The lot of the son-in-law in business is often an unhappy one. He accepts many belittlements as a means of obtaining substantial material benefits for his family and himself. He is often placed in a secondary status in the company, limited forever, despite his capabilities, because he is not of the blood."

Stern presents the following example of a typical client: "The father headed a prosperous service corporation in which his son and son-in-law had been active for several years. He considered Richard, the son-in-law, to be the most competent person in the company. He relied heavily on Richard's judgment in the business, and socially they were very close. Richard was considered to be the most responsible and understanding individual in the whole family. In fact, the father repeatedly said to friends that his son-in-law was just like a son, and that he found it easier to relate to him than to either his son, Morton, or his daughter and Richard's wife, Carol."

During an estate-planning session, Stern, being aware of his client's tax situation and of Richard's value to the company, suggested that his client give some stock to his capable son-in-law. The client flatly rejected the idea, saying, "What happens if Richard and Carol get divorced or Carol predeceases him? He will undoubtedly remarry and I don't want him as a stockholder if he is married to someone other than my daughter."

Stern comments: "His response was one that I have heard so many times. In truth, his commitment to Richard was premised on his being married to Carol. It did not run to Richard individually. The vesting of stock ownership in the name of the inactive daughter means the son-in-law is working for his wife. This is the reality that most sons-in-law face."

Curtis L. Carlson, CEO of Radisson Hotel Corporation—whose son-in-law has become his designated successor—adds, "You make more allowances for a family member. Instead of considering why a son-in-law should be promoted, what you look for is why he *shouldn't* be!"

Parent/owners are also sometimes wary of giving stock to married sons for fear the daughter-in-law would become a business partner in the event of a son's death unless adequate insurance and buy-back agreements are in place. In case of divorce, a daughter-in-law could lay claim to the financial value of stock owned by the son—and this could be a sticky matter for the family business to resolve.

Parent/owners need to understand that a daughter-in-law is a prisoner of conflicting loyalties. First and foremost come her husband and children. If her husband's commitment to the family business seems to be making him worn out and unhappy, she will find it hard to support his job demands, especially if she doesn't understand where the business is going and what it could eventually do for her family.

Often the daughter-in-law is perceived as an intruder into the business by other family members, especially if her husband is unhappy in the business. Other family members—especially the parent/owner—may find her a convenient scapegoat for their own frustrations and disappointments regarding the successor candidate's failure to perform.

The parent/owner often exacerbates this problem by cautioning the successor against sharing business problems with his wife. Or, the daughter-in-law may be insulated from the realities of the family business workplace, getting only the spouse's version. Either way, she becomes a prime candidate for the role of intruder or scapegoat by her own ignorance, mixed, of course, with her concern for her spouse's happiness.

Maintaining business confidentiality from spouses has been widespread until recent years. In fact, during the decade that Nat Shulman was in business with his older brother, he agreed wives should not be privy to business information because: "They wouldn't understand and it would create jealousy and tension."

(Even though, in Shulman's situation, the jealousy and tension were there, with or without information!)

In contrast, Shulman's successor-son's wife is privy to all sorts of the business's operational information. In fact, she wrote the employees' manual and actively attends national conventions and selected business meetings with Nat's son. She's smart, objective, and lends a great deal of support to him during many difficult business decisions. The Shulman family is simply lucky to have her attitude and ability at their disposal.

As this daughter-in-law's case illustrates, sharing operational business information with appropriate in-laws who are not actively participating in the business may go a long way toward achieving a healthy and effective successorship transition. An informed and balanced home environment can be of tremendous importance to successor candidates as they navigate the turbulent rapids of taking over control of the family business.

The secret to success in family business is to prevent the emotional dynamics of the family from causing wrongheaded business decisions. Nowhere is this more difficult than in dealing with in-law relationships, where the tendency is to be loyal to blood ties at the expense of potentially profitable and beneficial relationships with relatives by marriage. You can avoid this counterproductive tendency by being aware of the anxieties your sons- and daughters-in-law are experiencing; by awarding an in-law a position based on ability alone; and, finally, by making sure the in-law's continued success in the company is not contingent upon the success of the marriage.

Also, bear in mind that, in many cases, in-laws make better successor candidates than blood children, because—growing up outside the family circle—they have been spared all the emotional baggage and parental impact the parent/owner has had on his children. The image of a powerful and successful parent can have restricting and frustrating effect on a son or daughter in the dynamics of succession. An in-law has burdens to bear, but this particular problem is not one of them. The loyalty yoke that can block a child from making objective, businesslike decisions does not hang as heavily around the neck of the son- or daughter-in-law, and that can make them all the more valuable.

4. The Fast-Changing Role of Women

Evolution of a Neanderthal

For thirty years of Nat Shulman's business career, not once did it enter his mind that his daughter might join the family business. Under his biased rule, female members of the family were kept from knowing much about the operation of the business, and certainly were never considered for management positions. This attitude was carried over from Nat's ten-year stewardship as a junior partner to his older brother. While they worked together, they agreed their wives were not to be included in any discussions regarding the business. It was an accepted "fact" in those days that women would not understand business problems and would only "complicate things." Female employees in businesses were hired only to keep the offices running smoothly, and they generally earned less than the men.

Fortunately for Nat and his business, his Neanderthal mentality has gone the way of a good portion of his hair. The unlimited resources that women have brought to his family business as they've proved themselves to be top-notch managers and CEOs have converted him into a champion of the female family business member. He's not the only one, either. Women in Family Business, a nationwide group of daughters of business owners, started three years ago with five members and today has five hundred. Since the University of Pennsylvania's Wharton School began its family business program in 1982, female enrollment has doubled. Women now make up about 34 percent of the program.

Shulman's daughter Karen grew up in the traditional woman's role: She earned a degree in occupational therapy, married, and had a child. Ultimately, though, she became bored and disenchanted with her chosen path and interviewed for a sales representative position for Johnson & Johnson's Tylenol Division. This situation was akin to the ship's officer who interviewed for a job on the *Titanic*, for Karen won the job only to face heavy artillery during the infamous period when several bottles of Tylenol tablets were laced with cyanide. Business history has recorded the exemplary fashion in which Johnson & Johnson handled this crisis, and Nat's daughter was in the thick of it. In the meantime, though, her marriage faltered and she became a single parent. She accepted a full-time job with a large pharmaceutical company, progressing to a management position with a large salary.

Despite all this, her father was still blind to the talent and level of his daughter's professionalism. Even as he groomed his son, Scott, for successorship, his daughter was winning in the corporate jungle.

It was his son, in fact, who demanded that Nat evolve. Seeing how well his sister was handling herself in the business world, Scott pushed his father to make Karen the manager of one of the important divisions. Nat went to great lengths to discourage his son from involving Karen in the business, saying it would "foster complications" and that "she was doing very well where she was."

Incensed by his apparent lack of family loyalty, Scott finally shouted, "I want her in the business, no matter what you say!"

Nat replied, "Well, Scott, it's yours and Karen's decision—I hope it works out."

"It will!" he hollered. "She's damn good at what she does, and I want her here!"

As Shulman left his office, chastened and subdued, his pride in both his children overwhelmed him and he realized that they had just helped their very loving and caring, but rather stupid, father overcome a persistent prejudice. Such rewards of family business can make all the trouble and conflicts seem minor.

There are many chauvinist fathers in the family business world who severely limit their successor and managerial pools by never considering the female members of their families. In his *Inc.* magazine piece in August 1987, "Why Daughters Are Better," Curtis Hartman tells the story of a family business owner who contemplated selling his business when his only son showed no interest in it. When asked about his daughter's interest and aptitude, Hartman reports, the owner laughed derisively and asked him how she could bring up the grandchildren and run an entire company at the same time. "The shame of it is that he has another choice, if only he could see it," Hartman notes.

Sometimes it's the daughter who fails to see her potential role in the business. Cindy Ross had never considered working in the family's male-dominated crane-leasing business in Cleveland—until she saw female friends accept jobs in the industry. "Suddenly, I realized that I could be doing for my father what they were doing for other people," says Cindy, currently a vice-president of Ross Equipment Corporation. Demographic data gathered from Wharton students indicate that women in family businesses commonly have higher salaries, more responsibility, and greater ownership potential than their counterparts in other corporations, according to a *Wall Street Journal* article by Meg Sullivan. "For some women," Sullivan writes, "joining the family business may in fact be the best alternative."

Preferable Successors?

Although women have long worked in family businesses, usually the upper echelons have been closed to them. Succession traditionally has been granted to the eldest son, groomed virtually from birth to follow in his father's footsteps. According to Peter Davis of the Wharton School, it's still common for fathers to view their daughters as "Daddy's little girl" long after they have proven themselves in the business world. A father with no son who wanted to protect his daughter's financial interest typically hired not her but her husband.

As divorce rates soar, however, hiring in-laws for marriage-related reasons, instead of for what they can bring to the business, has become risky business. Many sons, meanwhile, feel less bound to tradition and are pursuing careers outside the family business. At the same time, women have become better educated and trained for management positions.

Considering daughters for management positions in the family business opens up an exciting new talent pool. In some respects, daughters are preferable successors. According to consultants, sons tend to go into the family business with desires to compete with the parent/owner, while daughters tend to go into the business to be closer to the parent. More importantly, according to Donald Jonovic, a Cleveland business consultant and author, "Most daughters didn't assume they were coming to work at the family business, so they went out and got outside experience."

A big plus for daughters is their capability to empathize with the parent's fear of letting go of power and control. Among sons, concern for the senior generation's mourning the love affair it has had with the business is generally not as high.

"Women are taught to be more nurturing, more attuned to emotional needs, and are socialized to express more concern with helping the family," says Matilde Salganicoff, a Philadelphia family business consultant and therapist who conducts workshops at Wharton. "Women generally go into business to help the family, and secondarily to develop a career. But sons don't go in primarily to help their fathers or their family—it's simply not their central theme."

These observations are not new; indeed, classical literature is filled with the tales of tragic confrontations between fathers and sons. Nonetheless, consideration for the feelings of the father/owner as he is facing his mortality and giving up his powerful role as leader of the business is a vital requisite for all successors. Male siblings would serve themselves well by emulating the more caring attitude often exhibited by their sisters. It's not only ethical, it's practical.

The traditional dream of adding "And Son" to the name of the company is going out of style along with the assumption the parent/owner of the business is always male. One of Joe's favorite CEO Club members heads a book distribution business in Boston. This father of four children, all daughters, has a dozen trucks on the road at all times. Painted on the side of the trucks is a picture of four daughters surrounding a father entitled "Murphy and Daughters," the name of the company. Not something you expect after seeing so many carpenter and plumbing trucks with "So-and-So & Sons" on the side.

Joe's wife, Karla, is the oldest child in a family business and was the heir-apparent from birth. Her dad, Karl, expected a son to take over the family business, Karl Schulz & Sons; but when his first child turned out to be female, he simply decided it didn't matter. In his view, the first one got the birthright, be it a Karl or a Karla.

In today's fast-moving and creative consumer-oriented marketplace, businesses that do not change to fit current needs go the way of the dinosaur. This same philosophy must be applied to the successorship challenge if family businesses are to survive with the family's control intact.

Women have proven they can "cut the mustard" in the family business workplace. This does not imply male members of the family are not capable. It simply means the sons' previous exclusive right to succeed Dad is no longer automatically given—anymore than it's a given these days that Dad and not Mom owns the business. Sons must earn this right alongside capable and talented sisters interested in the business.

This is a blessing, as the old "heir-apparent" attitude has been responsible for so many of the tragic scenarios that abound in family business successorships. Many sons with great talent outside the business world go into the family business because of feelings of obligation, and fail. Incompetent sons may be handed control as their "birthright" and may run the business into the ground. Unresolved personality conflicts and power struggles between sons and fathers tear families apart.

Automatic succession of male progeny should be removed from the successorship process and replaced by competition among all children for the future control of the family business. Beyond making the entire process more fair, this would provide the following benefits:

- It would remove a burdensome obligation from the back of an unwilling male successor who would rather do something else with his life.
- It would push male successors who grew up feeling that they were entitled to the business to shape up.
- It would open up successorship to an often neglected consideration that should actually be the most important factor in choosing a successor—choosing the best-qualified family member to be CEO.

Daddy's little girl may be a better choice than her brothers for successorship—better suited to the transition, better motivated, and often better trained, by dint of her outside experience. What's that feminist adage? "A woman has to work twice as hard as a man to be considered half as good." The extrahard work a daughter has to put in to be considered as successor may make her more assertive, goal-oriented, and successful. As Hartman writes, "Ask the management experts. Ask the psychologists. Better still, ask the fathers who have tried it. Nearly all agree that when it comes to succession, daughters are better."

Still, as always in the family business, communication is the key. If a competent, educated daughter lets her father know that she wants to be considered as a candidate early on, then they can work together to prepare her for the job. During the training period, Dad can learn to relate to her as a businesswoman and both can gain confidence in her abilities.

Working Mothers

A challenge for successor/daughters is childcare. Even unmarried, childless women must face the possibility that someday they may have to share their commitment to the business with this important distraction. On the flip side, as Debra Coffin, a new mother who gave up a promising legal career to enter her family's New Jersey business, notes: "Your boss is also the grandfather of your children. He not only understands if you take the afternoon off to attend a nursery-school graduation, he may even come along."

Nat Shulman was an almost daily witness to the extra responsibilities and pressures of a single parent as he watched his daughter, Karen, care for his young grandson. As he regularly stopped by her house for morning coffee, he watched her bustle about the kitchen with the phone tucked under her chin, stopping periodically to admonish her son to eat his breakfast. This was followed by a drop-off at the daycare center at the other end of town from her job. Her evening schedule began with picking him up at 5:30 P.M., which Shulman sometimes did after receiving a stressed-out call from a delayed mother.

Working mothers—even single mothers—with small children are a permanent fixture of our modern culture. No business can expect to be removed from the effects of female employees who need special attendance consideration because of the demands of their children. Recognizing the value of their female employees, progressive organizations have opened daycare centers on the premises, and have established "mother's hours" so working mothers can be home before the kids return from school.

The family business should prepare, as well, to assist female members with these responsibilities, rather than shunt them onto a "mommy track" or keep them out of the business altogether. If Daddy's little girl can handle the responsibilities of being a mother and still outperform her brother in the workplace, shouldn't the family business encourage her to reach for the top?

The New Wives—Informed

Wives of family business owners should know how the business operates even if they have nothing to do with it. Many family business owners deny their spouses—and often even their successors—access to confidential information about the business, trusting that in case of death or serious disability, the attorneys and accountants will fill the void.

This is all very well when dealing with the taxes and insurance proceeds, but it won't begin to answer the question of who can become the CEO and run the business on a day-to-day basis when the founder suddenly is incapacitated. Widows thrust into making decisions for a business about which they know very little may not be able to keep it going. At the absolute minimum, a spouse should know:

- What are the assets of the business and how much are they worth?
- How would I get a loan, if needed? Will I and the business qualify?
- How do I get cash in an emergency if my spouse is away or incapacitated?
- Will the children have money for college if our income drops?
- Where is my husband's will? What does it say?
- Where is his life insurance? What does it pay?

There are some good books on the market designed to help women answer these questions. *Answers* was written by Becky Barker after the unexpected death of her entrepreneur husband left her not only widowed but without knowledge even of where to find the key to his safe. According to Sandra Celli of DMA Group, a consultant firm for growing businesses, Becky's situation is not at all unusual. Her book comes with pockets for various documents (from the marriage certificate to funeral arrangements) so that a spouse could gain instant access to these should the need arise.

Another excellent resource is *A Survival Kit for Wives: How to Avoid Financial Chaos Before Tragedy Strikes,* by Don and Renee Martin. It features detachable worksheets for assembling vital information and describes what information to keep, where to keep it, as well as valuable advice on how to raise emergency cash and design long-term financial plans. Both of these books are available from Joe Mancuso's organization, as well as in bookstores. For a copy call or write: The Center for Entrepreneurial Management Inc., 180 Varick St., 17th floor, New York, NY 10014, (212) 633–0060.

Thirty years ago Nat Shulman witnessed a sad example of an unprepared wife, which might not have turned out so badly today. A friend of Nat's died unexpectedly, leaving his widow—an intelligent woman trained as an attorney—to figure out what to do with the automobile dealership. Their son, at seventeen, was too young to carry out his father's wish for him to take over the business, but pleaded with his mother not to sell the business. The best move may have been to sell the business and put the money in trust for the son, who could then use the money to enter the automobile business as a mature, trained young man.

Blinded by the pleadings of her immature son, the widow attempted to operate the business with the help of her husband's general manager, although she had never been included in the business and had minimal knowledge of it. The biggest problem was that the general manager's talent seemed to have been buried with her husband, and the business went bankrupt within a year and a half.

If this had happened today instead of thirty years ago, perhaps the dealer might have been eager to involve his bright wife in the daily operation of the business. Her legal training might have come in handy, and she could have been trained to take over the business and preserve it for their son. If you think such training is expensive, just consider the alternative, and training will look quite cheap.

Voluntary training of wives as successors is a revolutionary idea, but with all the statistics showing women outliving men, it certainly is a good, practical one. Such training should ideally take place during the forty- to fifty-five-year-old period, for during this time the spouse ordinarily would be free of the demands of small children. This notion does not, however, preclude the necessity for young business owners to share their work with spouses through attendance at business conventions, seminars, and workshops.

The old warning, "Don't bring the office home with you," may not be in the best interest of the modern marriage. Marriages today often resemble partnerships more than the melding of two individuals into one—as they did a generation ago. Today's woman is both interested in what her husband does during his workday and eager to share her work experience with her husband. Even if the business is highly technical and a full understanding of it would require special training, a spouse can still be taught how the organization works. A basic knowledge of the business's finances and how they affect the family should be shared, too.

If you do put your spouse on the payroll, there is a right way and wrong way to do it. The right way provides tax benefits; the wrong way can be more trouble than it is worth. Follow these five simple steps, from Boston CEO Club member John Schortmann's *Business Incorporated,* a tax, financial, and estate planning information sheet for corporate business owners:

- Treat your spouse like any other employee, paying the going rate for someone doing the same work.
- Make sure your spouse fills out a time sheet regularly.
- Pay your spouse by check through your business account, just as you would any employee.
- Be certain to deduct the correct amount of federal, state, and local taxes from your spouse's wages. Send a W-2 form for the year to your spouse.
- File the appropriate forms with the IRS when they are due (e.g., Form W-3 and Form 941).

According to Schortmann, as long as you follow the above steps, you should be able to take the following tax deductions:

1. Reimbursement to the spouse for family medical and dental expenses.
2. Travel and entertainment expenses incurred for business purposes.
3. The payment of the $50,000 death benefit to you in the event your spouse dies.
4. Group term life insurance protection for your spouse (up to $50,000 coverage is tax-free).
5. Pension or profit-sharing or Keogh plan distributions if you are self-employed.
6. Contributions by your spouse to an IRA (deductible only within certain limits).
7. Accident insurance on your spouse.
8. Home office expenses (limited).
9. Meal monies paid to your spouse for working through the dinner hour.
10. Tuition and education travel reimbursements (assuming the education improves your spouse's skills needed in the business).

These tips are useful for spouses of both sexes. As we write, about 25 percent of the CEO Club members are married women, and their ranks are growing. By the time you read this book, the ratio might be fifty-fifty.

Mom—The Referee

Mothers traditionally have played a mediator's role in the family business. If well informed, a mother can serve as an effective clearinghouse for all sorts of valuable information for family business participants. If poorly informed, though, Mom is likely to become a mere depository for gripes and gossip. When included in business decisions and discussions, however, mothers are often in a unique position to bridge the gap between business and family values, thus promoting the adoption of policies that are not only effective but fair and keep people happy.

Many mothers whose families are in business wield a great deal of power and influence. For this reason alone, mothers should be kept abreast of how people are interacting in the workplace; they should not rely only on one-sided reports.

This may seem to be a minor point, but in the family business environment, disasters can develop when even one person is misinformed.

Nat was called in as a consultant a few years ago by Charlie Blackwell, a seventy-year-old new-car dealer with a son and son-in-law in his business. He was spending more and more time enjoying himself on the golf course, but was concerned that any problems with the business be cleared up before he retired completely.

As Nat's team explored the operation of the business, it became glaringly apparent that the immature twenty-nine-year-old son and the capable forty-two-year-old son-in-law had a problem with each other. The son-in-law was general manager, and had Charlie's complete confidence. The son was new-car sales manager, and his lack of commitment to the job was clearly responsible for low sales. The son-in-law seemed to be sincerely trying to motivate the son, but could not get past the son's resentment of him and the lazy attitude he had developed as "heir-apparent."

The son-in-law soon admitted that unless this conflict was resolved, he was going to resign and set up a dealership of his own in another state. His wife, the owner's daughter, heartily supported this tack, although it would mean moving further away from her parents.

The solution was to give the son—temporarily—a less responsible management position and continue his training. Charlie agreed his son should invest a few more years in learning the business—enabling him to mature professionally—so the family could stay together in the business. He was eager to keep his daughter and grandchildren close by.

Up to this point, nobody had heard from Charlie's wife of forty-two happy years, Janet. Charlie had always sheltered her from any business problems, including those he had been having with their son in the workplace. Her son, on the other hand, hadn't hesitated to give her his one-sided version of the facts. Subsequently, when all the negative reports about him came in, she reacted like a mother bear fighting for her cub. Her little boy was being "pushed out of the business," she said, complaining, "everything was perfect until those consultants came along and shook everyone up."

Charlie backed down, the son-in-law finally resigned and opened his own dealership five hundred miles away, and the son continued to be a mediocre new-car sales manager. Charlie was forced to leave the golf course and go back to running the dealership, severely impairing the successorship process.

If he had not sheltered Janet from the business, she might have cooperated with the plans—knowing of the problems her son was having. Instead, Charlie's old-fashioned protective attitude toward "the little woman" collapsed his house of cards. Sensitive decisions like those faced by the Blackwell family require everyone to be informed. Ignorance of what makes a business successful, accompanied by parental protectiveness, can be devastating—however unlikely it may be for some parents to stop overprotecting their children. As women continue to exhibit their business acumen, it is sound practice for male owners to share operational information with their spouses. The same advice should be heeded by female family business owners.

Unfortunately, history tells us that husbands and wives sometimes become adversaries during the successor's candidacy for management and control of the family business. It has even been reported that one mother hired a hit man to kill her husband because she was angry about how he was treating their son in the workplace.

Trying to change how mothers and fathers view their children is a difficult battle; the handling of information about the business is less delicate. The sharing of operational information between spouses is crucial. A spouse who has always known what's going on can serve well as a mediator throughout the history of the business and can be especially useful during the inevitable conflicts which arise between the owner and the successor candidate.

For this reason, macho men should acknowledge the old adage: "The hand that rocks the cradle, rules the world," and include their wives as informed business partners and advisers. Psychologists enthusiastically support daughters, wives, and mothers as successors. Mothers as competent successorship advisers deserve our encouragement, also.

5. Outside Advisers

We are about to tell a memorable story that should provide the impetus for creating a real board of advisers for any business and most especially for a family business. The real reason the outside board can be so valuable has as much to do with the makeup of the creator/founder/entrepreneur as it does with the inherent wisdom of the advice. Having an outside group of advisers (you don't have to call them a board) can be the best thing you ever do, PERIOD.

In a family business, this independent voice can save not only the business, but the family too. That's why it's doubly vital.

MR. INSIDE—MR. OUTSIDE

One of the greatest Army football teams in history had two great running backs in Glenn Davis and Doc Blanchard. Part of their greatness lay in the fact that each manifested a unique talent. One excelled in running plays through the line, the other was outstanding in going around the ends. The media graphically referred to them as "Mr. Inside" and "Mr. Outside."

This sports example is valuable in demonstrating how most successful businesses achieve excellence by combining inherent talents of associates. For a moment, think about the great combinations of a "Mr. Inside" and "Mr. Outside" that you have experienced in your business career—maybe even in your own business.

Below is a framework for an entrepreneur to pick a first mate. You know, the number-one employee, the one who replaces you when your car breaks down.

OK? Or the one who has a personality trait that may supplement a deficiency in your own character—not one that you're conscious of, perhaps. Which of the four choices below is optimum for you?

	Bright	*Stupid*
Energetic	3	2
Lazy	4	1

Choice 1 (Stupid and Lazy). We both know that this choice is a loser, so let's not dwell on it. After all, these folks don't really belong in private business, do they?

Choice 2 (Energetic and Stupid). Again, this one is a loser. Actually it's worse than choice 1. The energetic part can really hurt. They love to write memos and call meetings to hear themselves babble on. But, believe it or not, neither of these two choices (1 and 2) are the worst of the four options.

By the way, those energetic and stupid types seem to gravitate naturally to politics. They don't seem to stand out as different among that crowd.

Choice 3 (Bright and Energetic). You probably already guessed it (see how bright and energetic you are?): the worst choice is 3. It can actually destroy the business.

There is nothing worse than two captains of a ship, two leaders of the symphony, or two bosses. You see, entrepreneurs are bright/energetic and they naturally like other B/Es. So they often kill the business by selecting them to be their first mate. It's like using gasoline to put out a fire. Let us show you why this is the worst choice.

What does choice 1 (Lazy and Stupid) cost you? Actually, it's only his salary. It's a cheap mistake. Choice 2 (Energetic and Stupid) costs you the salary . . . plus damages. But, again, it will not put you out of business. Choice 3 (Bright and Energetic) can collapse the business. Now, let's hurry on to analyze our favorite choice.

Choice 4 (Bright and Lazy). Bless this type, because in combination with an entrepreneur, they can create ongoing businesses. When the Ready-Fire-Aim type gives them an order or tells them to hurry up and do something . . . they take their own sweet time about getting the task done. Sometimes they put it off for a day or two.

The beauty of this fact is that when the entrepreneur changes the marching instructions (they'll do it *every* time), they don't have to stop what they are doing to adjust. You see, as you get buffered you get better, and these B/Ls are really great buffers.

All of this is to show you the value of an outside board of advisers. Another buffer group. And an even better one.

An entrepreneur who has chosen a bright and lazy as a first mate needs only to complete the process by selecting a board of advisers. This combination (organizationally above and below the CEO) provides a warm cocoon of talent to nuture the decision-making process.

Outside Advisers

Engaging the average American family in an intense business relationship with each other would be a serious challenge to a professional counselor, so it's hardly surprising that it's difficult for the typical entrepreneurial family. One of the prime reasons for this is that underlying problems (such as a lack of accounting expertise, inadequate business information systems, and inefficient cash management), are tolerated in a family business to a greater degree than nonfamily organizations because of the close emotional ties of the players. This creates additional stress.

It is also common for the parent/founder to be so wrapped up in the business that the sons and daughters never learn to run the business. As a result, without the aid of outside consultants and advisers, the business left to itself will outgrow the family's capabilities. Just as poverty is a common result of doing nothing, chaos is the result of doing nothing in a family business.

The founding of the business was a lonely job. No one told you how to design it for efficiency. You mucked around yourself until it came together.

If, after years of struggling, you find it actually working and even being successful, you may be seduced into becoming too comfortable with your own limitations. This is when you may begin to manage by habit (erroneously referring to it as experience). Habits fall into two categories—good and bad—and it's often very difficult to objectively tell the difference. Personal confrontations between family business members also have the potential to destroy the business (and the emotional well-being of the family as well). Failure to resolve these tensions can be catastrophic! The penicillin for both of these diseases is to seek out competent advisers.

When you read our final chapter (which we purposely saved for last so that you'd dine on the appetizers and main course before you linger on the dessert), you will discover some of the families that fell out over this issue (Binghams, Guccis, Johnsons) waited too long to develop an outside independent influence. When both sides are firmly entrenched in an adversarial position, it's always too late. The time to establish a board of directors, outside management consultants, or specialized family business counselors is before emotions run out of control.

This idea is somewhat opposite to entrepreneurial logic. When things are apparently going smoothly, why change them? If it ain't broke, it don't need fixin'. But that's not true in family business. Like raising money for the business, the best time to raise capital is when you are not trapped in a lack-of-capital emergency. Although it sounds illogical at first, it is actually logical. The best time to establish an outside board of directors is when the family and the business are running well. That way, the directors can get grounded on both the family and the business and help to avoid a crisis, not try to solve a war. But entrepreneurs, by their nature, will always choose to beg for forgiveness rather than ask permission. And that is often the underlying cause of family business problems. It is also the one trait that is simultaneously a huge asset and a liability.

The premier architect and builder of the family business relationship is the parent/owner. This member of the team is the one who initially needs to acknowledge the value of outside advice and help, and to set the wheels in motion for it to happen. Unfortunately, in many cases it is the parent/owner who is the major obstacle to this happening.

Fundamentally, there are three major problems between family business members that may result in serious trouble.

First is the unwillingness of the parent/owner to acknowledge the maturity and talent of successor candidates, and to share the operational control of the business with them. Exacerbating this uneasiness is the parent/owner's anxiety of beginning to see the end of their many years of unilaterally running the business and being faced with retirement. This can be frightening to many entrepreneurs. Consequently, entrepreneurs such as Armand Hammer (Occidental Petroleum) stay too long at the helm of the business they created. Hammer was in his nineties when he finally gave up control of his enterprises.

Second, unqualified and unmotivated successor candidates join the family business because they feel obligated to the parent/owner to carry on the business, or they perceive a career in the family business as their birthright. Often, these family members will ignore special personal talents and career choices either to please or placate a dynamic parent/owner, or simply to take the easiest and fastest path to financial security.

Nat Shulman has personal experience with the latter: "Following my Navy service in World War II, I passed up an opportunity for a free college education under the GI bill to go into the automobile business with an older brother. At that time, I also forsook my lifelong desire to become a journalist in order to speed up my timetable for financial security. Fortunately, I was able to accomplish my goal for reasonable financial security and to also 'grab the brass ring' on my writing career, but the price of this decision was steep. I spent ten years of my life in a miserable situation as 'the boss's kid brother,' followed (fortunately) by twenty-five years in my own business."

Third, and most important, is the qualified and motivated successor candidate who cannot overcome the organizational and community obstacles of being the boss's son or daughter because of the lack of real support and commitment from the parent/owner. The parent often second-guesses and submarines their decisions, which erodes their effectiveness in the business, especially with other employees.

Outside advisers take many forms. Some may be formally involved (such as management consultants) or they may assume a more subtle posture as manager/mentors, long-term business associates or just plain friends. Family members who are not actively involved in the business (mothers or respected mature siblings) can significantly influence behavior in the business. However, it is risky to assume that this latter type of intervention can be effective. Rather, it should be regarded as a fortunate plus if and when it occurs. If there is a personal family problem affecting the well-being of the business, then traditional business measures should be used to correct it.

Performance accountability is the goal in any business, but often parent/owners are not capable of making these demands on their progeny, without a lot of family stuff getting in the way. Also, the parent/owner may have been so busy during the past few decades busting butt to build the business, doing whatever it took to survive and prosper, that the company has become *his* company, designed and constructed to fit his personality and modus operandi. And, while an apple doesn't fall far from the tree, it does fall off the tree. Is it any wonder, then, that any intrusion (like successor candidates) on this dictatorial process has a difficult, if not often impossible, time making the case for transition? This task is best handled by involving unemotional and objective third parties.

One of the most effective accountability measures for CEOs is to establish an outside board of directors (or advisers) recruited from the business community who are *not* exclusively connected with the business as family members or company accountants and attorneys. The board members meet at *regular* intervals and are paid a fee for their involvement. It's good business practice.

This type of board is not to be confused with the perfunctory types popular among smaller corporations, in which nonactive family members and others who serve in name only are listed in order to conform to the law.

Leon Danco, family business consultant with the Center for Family Business in Cleveland, believes so strongly in the value of outside boards of directors that he has coauthored with Donald Jonovic an entire book on the subject, *Outside*

Directors in the Family Business (published by the University Press of Cleveland, Ohio). Dr. Danco writes, "No well-run business, family owned or not, can operate efficiently over any extended period of time without a periodic review of both the actions of its executive officers and the policies they pursue to meet the challenge of the future. And the body best designed to deliver this review is the board of directors." He continues, "Every conscientious CEO needs a competent working board of outside directors to serve as his/her challenger, supporter (especially important to successor candidates), and enforcer, as well as his/her conceptualizer, arbiter, and monitor. This kind of board *can* be a yardstick by which the CEO *can* measure himself, his goals, his responsibilities, and his actions.

"Disagreements inevitably arise between parent/owners and their designated manager–successors. The differences in outlook, management style, and objectives are usually significant. In companies without outside directors, these disagreements are usually resolved in Dad's favor—not necessarily because he is right, but surely because he holds all the chips. If this happens often enough, disagreements become conflicts and the transition is in trouble."

For many high-powered titans of industry, management decisions fall into the following categories: *their* way and the *wrong* way. A meaningful outside board of directors is an excellent antibiotic for this common malaise, which reduces potentially talented organizations to "rubber-stamp" mediocrity. Above all, the most important reason for legitimate boards of directors is the accountability they demand from the family CEO. Often, the family value system gets in the way of basic, objective, sensible business decisions. New-generation family CEOs may take regressive liberties with company management and fiscal policies because of a forgiving attitude of an indulgent parent/owner. The legitimate Board will not permit this to happen.

Conversely, if the parent/owner is unfairly and unwisely withholding management opportunities from a capable family member successor candidate to the detriment of the business, then the outside board can assume a position of championing the cause of the oppressed family member.

Nat Shulman has such a story. "I have had personal experience, both as a kid brother and as a parent/owner, dealing with a highly motivated, talented successor candidate.

"I know the debilitating feeling of having an older brother/owner enter a room where I was conducting a meeting. He would sit down, look repeatedly at his watch, raise his hand, and innocently ask, 'May I say something?' At which point my control of the meeting evaporated, and subsequently the respect of long-term employees when other similar intrusions occurred during the day.

"On the other side of the coin, as a parent/owner, I had second-guessed my son so often and debilitated his management efforts to the point where he threatened to quit. I kept promising to stay out of his hair, but I kept slipping into 'innocent' questioning of his decisions until finally he and I reached a serious successorship impasse. Our business relationship was in danger of being terminated.

"Here we discovered another effective group of outside advisers for the challenges of family business transition problems. It is the management consultant firm whose primary function is to monitor and advise on the total operation of the business.

"Like so many times in life, this help for us came from a totally unexpected source. We had experienced some major problems with our service department and had retained the DMA Group from Exeter, New Hampshire to analyze our whole organization. After several weeks of investigation, they found that the single biggest problem in our organization was the relationship between my son and me. The managers and employees didn't know who was the boss!

"After an emotionally charged conference with Dick Caravati, the DMA senior consulting member, I was finally told that there was no way they could effectively resolve our organizational problems unless (A) I actually resigned as president and CEO and became chairman of the board in an advisory capacity, and (B) my son was appointed president and CEO, and also became the franchisee on our selling agreement with General Motors. My position would be solely as financial participant and consultant.

"This decision to step aside was not an easy one for me, even though I was sixty years old, in good health, and had developed nonfinancial interests in several other activities outside the business. After all, wasn't I in the prime of my life? I was enrolled in college seeking a degree, and my talented son's commitment to the daily operation of our successful and profitable Chevrolet dealership was far greater than mine.

"I eventually realized the best interests of the business would be served only if I accepted these recommended changes.

"The important message is that the confrontational problems between us would not have been resolved without the cool, objective, unemotional, and trained intervention by our management consulting team. In reality, a state of war existed in our family business with the two top generals feuding for power and control. It took cool, emotionally uninvolved trained-in-business professionals to negotiate the peace.

"I agreed to step aside and to permit my son to run the company without interference, with the proviso that they (DMA) would assume the responsibility for providing experienced counsel to him. They had an excellent long-term track record with family businesses all over the country, and I was comfortable they could 'fill in the holes' where I thought my son might be light on experience. The cost amounted to what it would have been for one additional manager, with which I was very comfortable.

"There is no question in my mind that this particular form of outside advisory help saved my son's and my business relationship. And furthermore, their business management expertise has paid off handsomely on our bottom line. It's a win-win arrangement. The primary responsibility of these firms *is* to improve the profitability of the business, thereby making their services cost-effective. However, a major part of their attention is focused on the business's human resources inventory and how it impacts the total performance of the organization.

"It is during this human resources evaluation that family members' interaction problems will surface and cry out for resolution, as ours did."

Many parent/owners have unique methods of manifesting their personal control tactics. Shulman tells of a parent/owner of a sizable hardware store whose first action upon returning from an extended absence was to rearrange several of the display items on the shelves (even though most of the current arrangements had been his doing!). He was simply letting everyone in the store know he was back.

Shulman's son recently related how much he dreaded those times when Nat returned from a trip and went through reconnecting rituals. Nat's personal control-shtick is an obsession with having all the cars on display in the yard (several hundred) parked with the front wheels straight. An interesting sidelight was a comment his son made about the straight wheels. He said, "The day before your scheduled return to the dealership, there were not too many cars sold because everybody was so preoccupied with straightening the front wheels on the displayed cars!"

In the years during which Shulman has examined and researched the family business experience, this scenario of parent/owners granting counterfeit authority in the business to successor candidates is one of the most widespread problems.

Many parent/owners reading the aforementioned struggle might assume that similar tensions do not exist in their businesses. The truth is, as a loving, caring parent, you may be innocently creating a living hell for your successor, and not even know it!

Outside Advisers Take Many Forms

Several major U.S. universities have established Family Business Institutes, which offer workshops as well as competent consultants, some available for individual counseling, including the Wharton School of the University of Pennsylvania; the University of Oregon; Loyola University; and Washington & Lee University.

One additional point about outside advisers: Once you have your circle of advisers in place, don't blow it by using them improperly. Don't set them against each other by getting in the habit of always consulting them separately. If you get an opinion on something from your lawyer and then call your accountant with, "Well, but Jeff said . . . ," they're going to waste a lot of time piecing things together. Meet with all of them together often enough so that they're all getting the same information, and acting in concert. This so-called little problem happens quite often.

Nonfamily advisers and mentors who are within the business organization also often assume important roles in the healthy continuation of the business. With nonfamily mentors, the important ingredient is the willingness of the parent/owner to invite managers and long-term employees to participate in the nurturing process of the successor candidate. While the parent/owner may be reluctant to involve managers and other employees in the training of the fledgling entrepreneur, it may reduce the feeling within the organization that the new generation is a threat to their future.

Sharing the training of the future CEO with capable managers will eliminate many of the bizarre assumptions by long-term employees over the emergence of the new generation of owner/management and its effect on their personal careers with the company. Firm commitments made by the owner addressing the future of the manager in the context of the successor also can help the situation.

As mentioned, the most important ingredient is to be candid and forthright and not leave anything open for assumption in agreements between the owner and the manager. Historically, the most-often used expression during serious disagreements is "I assumed." And we all know the word Assume makes an Ass of U and Me.

Other nonfamily advisers may include traditional business consultants, such as attorneys, accountants, insurance agents, bankers, state and national industry associations, plus industry management seminars and management groups. Here are some comments on each of these advisers:

1. *Attorneys.* A family business needs attorneys who are current on government regulations (as they pertain to your industry) and can readily translate them into "shoulds and shouldn'ts." They should also be well-versed in succession plans, management transfers, and the entire field of estate planning, including taxes.

   Just as the medical profession has become highly specialized, so it is with lawyers. Especially with tax questions, you should seek the best advice and counsel you can afford. There are few bargains with tax lawyers. You get what you pay for, and this is one place where the money you pay for competent tax lawyers may save several times their fees in saved taxes.

The best way to obtain good legal service might be to retain a reputable law firm rather than an individual attorney. The law firm has the capability to offer specialists; individual attorneys may be limited. If your law-firm attorney doesn't have the answer, then he'll have a partner who does. The best source of referrals for these lawyers is other CEOs who have good things to say about their legal firms.

2. *Accountants.* If your accountant is an old school chum who has done your books for several years, and if your staff is very comfortable with him, then you have cause for concern. "Feel-good accountants" lack the competency to demand financial discipline from your family business staff. Historically, family businesses are loosely run organizations because of the family's forgiving influence. This makes it doubly important that you retain "a bright, narrow-lapelled, white shirt, buttoned-down CPA who works for a first-class firm," as Leon Danco puts it in his book *Beyond Survival.* "One who will analyze the fiscal needs of your business and translate them into forecasts, budgets, monthly financial statements, year-end analysis and projections for the ensuing year, cost accounting systems and other cost controls, all of which are extremely necessary and valuable to management."

   A common scenario in family businesses is the aging accountant who has been doing the books since the business started and is immune from the winds of change so long as the parent/owner is around. If some of these parent/owners realized what this misplaced loyalty to old buddies was costing them in lost tax and operational savings, they would not be so tolerant!

3. *Insurance agents.* Here again is an example of how many family businesses may get enmeshed in the "old-boy network," dealing with unmotivated advisers because of long-term personal relationships with parent/owners.

   There is a myth that all insurance premiums cost the same. Untrue! Not only do the insurance premiums vary, but more importantly, the methods used to place coverage can result in significant savings.

   The vast majority of insurance agents are competent and will efficiently service your business. However, there are some who become complacent and need to be placed periodically in a competitive bidding position to keep them sharp. Also, there are costly pitfalls in the manner in which insurance companies may assess charges to your company. It behooves you to demand constant surveillance of your account by your agent. For example: Your firm reports a serious workers compensation injury to your insurance company. Soon after partial benefits and medical bills are paid to the claimant, the insurance company sets up a reserve for what they estimate the total cost of the claim will be. (These estimates are seldom conservative.) This reserve amount is promptly factored into your experience modification, thereby increasing your premium. Even if the insurance company does not pay out a dime on this reserve, you will not get a subsequent credit for unused reserves. Equally important are the companies that are not too prompt in removing the reserves from your experience modification, and unless your agent keeps the insurance company's feet to the fire, these costly reserves can hang around for a couple of years.

One further note: Make sure that your insurance agent has the versatility to be able to place your coverage with several companies. Often, an individual insurance company will decide for some unexplained reason to discontinue doing business with certain industries. There may be no rational explanation and this should not significantly affect your insurance coverage or cost, if your agent is on the ball. Also, in recent years, a new form of insurance adviser has come on the scene. This is the pure insurance consultant who does not work on commission but instead charges a fee to search the market for the best insurance deal for your company. Periodically using this type of service can provide insights into many other insurance coverage opportunities, as well as cost savings.

4. *Bankers.* When dealing with bank officials, it is important to assess the clout of your particular contact in the bank. Often, assistant vice-presidents or branch managers may be simply messengers to bring your requests to a loan officer or any other senior officer. If possible, try to present your proposition personally to someone who can make a decision, or who may need only board approval for your loan.

   Also keep in mind that the bank has several customer interest rates, so these rates are negotiable. They will try hard to get you to personally endorse or guarantee the loan. This is not written in stone. If your deal is minimally leveraged, you should not have to personally endorse the note. Tell them to buzz off!

   This might shock you, but in Shulman's experience (forty years in the new-car business), he claims he never received good "visionary" advice from a banker. Unless he/she is the senior economist for a major bank, don't expect entrepreneurial words of wisdom from your average banker.

Bankers are programmed to loan money at a profit and to see that it's repaid, and their primary concern is for their depositors and the bank examiners.

There is no question that establishing a relationship with an aggressive banker is important if your business is going to prosper and grow. Just remember that you are the one who has a finger on the pulse of the market. The banker is bound by fiduciary responsibility to the depositors (and the state bank examiners) to loan money with minimum risk and maximum guarantees.

5. *Industry Association Seminars and Management Groups* (20 Clubs). Because most of Shulman's business career was spent as a retail new-car dealer, he has grown to value the various national and state automobile trade association training and advisory groups that are available to new-car dealers. You should be able to assess the availability of similar opportunities in your particular industry. *Mancuso's CEO Clubs* around the country, composed of CEOs running businesses with about $20 million in annual sales, are another good group to interact with for ideas. Check with your particular trade association to see what advisory and consulting services they offer.

6. The Successorship Struggle

Successorship Doesn't Come Naturally

An oft-quoted statistic is that 60 percent of American family businesses fail to pass successfully to the next generation; closer to 75 percent fail to make it to the third generation. For too many business owners, passing down the family business to a son or daughter simply means taking care of all the estate, legal, and tax matters. This is less than half of the task, however. If the heirs are expected to operate the business, serious attention must be paid to their training and empowerment. If you think training is expensive, just measure the cost of ignorance.

One of the heavy prices for possession of wealth is the hassle and responsibility of allocating it properly in advance of death by writing a proper will. This is an unpleasant task, easily put out of one's mind—along with thoughts of "the end"—once completed. The family business owner, though, cannot just allocate his legacy and then depart for the higher realms if he really expects his business to survive. While barely past his prime, he must act daily to ensure that it continues beyond his lifetime by choosing, training, and eventually handing the business over to his successor.

Many family business owners have not seriously addressed successorship by their fifties or even sixties for the following reasons:

- They don't want to face the fact that their lives and careers are finite. Confronting the successorship process reinforces this unpleasant reality daily.

- The owner, the only one capable of kickstarting the process, is so busy with the operational demands of the business that he just never gets around to it.

The first step toward a successful successorship must be to realize that letting go of the management and control of a business that has been the core of his adult life is going to be very difficult for the owner. Not only is he letting go of his main preoccupation but by training a successor—a robust, competent, and autocratic entrepreneur—he is admitting that his career and life are indeed finite. These Godlike creatures are human after all!

The second step is to recognize that preparing the family business for perpetuity requires as much attention as constructing codicils in an estate plan and addressing inheritance tax issues. If the business is the most important asset in the estate, it will continue to generate profits and benefits for the family only to the degree to which the successors have been coached to use their talents and skills. Now do you see why training is cheaper than its alternative?

This is a heavy burden for any human being, let alone a results-oriented, fast-moving competitor who craves winning and lacks patience with incompetency. He must refine his simplistic methods for winning in the marketplace into the methods of a teacher, even though he has done minimal teaching and would probably not be good at it. Perhaps it is because they tend to be creative, or perhaps they are too self-centered, or too busy. Whatever the reason, teaching is not the entrepreneur's forte.

The same problem shows up in the sports world. A good player does not necessarily make a good manager. The skills needed to be a good manager are not the same skills needed to be a good player. And, in business, the skills needed by an entrepreneur are opposite to the skills needed to coach a successor candidate into the top job.

In addition, a parent who has seen his children as tots and teenagers, and carries all the accompanying memories of their childhoods, will not be able to prevent these deep primal impressions from influencing his relationship with them in the business environment. One business parent may make heavy demands of time and commitment of the aspiring successor, while another may be much less demanding and act like a traditional forgiving parent—rationalizing and accepting poor performance and tolerating low levels of commitment. Either extreme can have a lethal effect on the successorship process, as well as the family business.

If the expectations of a parent/owner are unreasonable and place demands on the successor far beyond the limits of other managers and employees, the successor may simply give up. If the parent/owner is constantly badgering the fledgling future CEO, this will have a negative effect on the entire organization, as employees exposed to this conflict will build resentments toward the owner and lose respect for the successor. In such a climate, all parties might be best served if the successor found another position in a similar business where he could gain experience and build confidence.

Conversely, if there is a lack of discipline and structure in the training process and little attention is paid to the successor's work habits, then the results will be poor. Employees will be unwilling to support such a successor when he is finally running the business. Latent talents of the candidate may atrophy and he may be lulled into a false sense of security, and, when the first emergency comes, he won't be ready.

Besides being the unwitting victims of their parent/owner's neuroses, aspiring successor candidates must deal with many of their own on their journey toward assuming control of the family business:

- They may be trapped by a sense of obligation to the family and be unsure of their desire to participate in the business.
- They must deal with resentment from long-term employees.
- They may experience intense competition and jealousy from other participating siblings and their spouses.
- They may become obsessed with proving themselves as they seek to carve out an identity in the parent's omnipresent shadow, and may become regressively defensive when interacting with the parent in the business.

In addition, the successor must deal with the resentment of long-term employees, intense competition, and jealousy from siblings and their spouses. He must also address the challenge of dealing with The Boss, after years of a traditional parent/child relationship, in a dramatically different way.

Closing the Value Gap: Third-Party Intervention

Upon objectively assessing the whirlwind of human dynamics set into play when the successorship process begins, it becomes very clear that the entire process clamors for professional attention.

First, the values of a family are different from those of a business. The family goal is to create happy, healthy humans, and though there may be a sincere effort toward harmony in the workplace, the ultimate goal for a business is simply to grow and make a profit. Family members are bound together via genealogy, love, and loyalty, while business members are bound by results and profitability, as well as degrees of loyalty mandated by contractual agreements. Families provide a protective environment in which parents can shield children from the rigors of life and siblings can protect each other from outsiders despite intrafamily rivalries. Penalties for ineffectiveness as a family member are usually only verbal criticism and negative attitudes from other family members. There is usually an abundance of tolerance for human frailties, while the business environment can be unforgiving, cold, hard, and only about survival and winning. Room for failure and ineptitude is minimal and they are swiftly addressed. Timing and performance, two elements of little importance to family relationships, are crucial to the survival of a business.

It seems safe, therefore, to assume that a major reason why the majority of family businesses do not survive beyond the third generation, or even the second, *is that the human dynamics of families and of businesses are incompatible and, indeed, can debilitate each other.* It is no wonder personality conflicts and human misery emerge from countless family businesses.

There are no miracle drugs for the malaise that affects family members trying to operate a business together. The basic problems of each may be the same, but there are hundreds of variations on these problems and countless other dynamics affecting each participant. The important first step, however, is to recognize that a healthy successorship will not come naturally and that communication and planning are essential.

Fortunately, the last decade has seen a dramatic increase in the emphasis on human resources management for American businesses, with an attendant emphasis on communication and human resource development.

This new focus on the people inventory of a business has been a tremendous advantage to family members who are becoming involved in the family business. The more attention that is directed toward the human element and communication in the workplace, the more professionalism that will be directed toward the relationships of family members in that environment.

In our chapter on outside advisers (chapter 5), we discuss several techniques available to family businesses to develop that professionalism. All three can be helpful for picking and/or preparing a successor:

- Create a creditable board of director/advisers removed from the emotional dynamics of the family that can support objective, healthy decisions.
- Allow a trusted senior manager to act as a mentor and buffer for the successor candidate.
- Retain a reputable management consulting firm to guide players in the successorship scenario and, in the process, work on the bottom line.

The most important step is to get family members to acknowledge the existing emotional dynamics and deal objectively with them. This is not an easy task. It may require some major attitude changes by all parties if the successorship process is going to address the requirements of the business without causing irreparable damage to the family. Third-party intervention may be crucial to a palatable resolution. Unfortunately, the use of third-party assistance is sidestepped by many misguided family business owners because the only one with the power to initiate the process will not admit there is a problem.

In fact, one of the most common tragedies in the successorship process is the parent/owner who is "beating up" on the successor and will not recognize any problem. There may be no problem so far as the parent/owner is concerned, for things are well under his control and power. The problems he refuses to recognize are those of a business associate (who also happens to be a family member) who is frustrated at not being allowed to reach his potential until the "old man" decides, or dies. The successor candidate may simply resign and go somewhere else to work.

Darn few business owners can successfully negotiate the turbulent and demanding waters of the successorship rapids without outside assistance. Be it in the form of a close business associate acting as an adviser or intermediary, an outside board of directors, a capable manager/mentor or an independent management consulting firm, outside help is necessary to preserve both the family and business relationships. Successor relationships deteriorate without it.

The Transfer of Power and Control

Any separation from an intimate relationship is sad. Usually such separations are involuntary, caused by death or other forces beyond human control. Departure from a life's work (except when it's due to death) is painful in part *because* it is voluntary and because we must take full responsibility for every step of making it happen. This takes a great deal of strength of character and an even larger measure of love and caring.

While working with dozens of successor candidates and their parents at the CEO Club's three-day Family Business Experience, a basic common theme emerged: Successors confessed they were debilitated by the reluctance of their parents to let go, while the parent/owners emphatically assured us that the management transition of their business was progressing satisfactorily and that they "had no problem!"

When one participant has no problem while the other complains about the process, there is probably a serious problem for everybody.

One of our interviews was with a successful multifranchise car dealer who is so involved in the daily operation of his dealership that his friends joke that when he dies, he will probably make Saint Peter a deal for his chariot as he passes through the pearly gates. This dealer has a fine, intelligent, ambitious son in his thirties who is sincerely committed to the business.

When we questioned this sixty-seven-year-old dealer about his plans for transferring control of the business to his son, he said, "Why do you make such a big deal out of turning over the business to the kid? My kid is doing a heck of a job, and loving every minute of it! I've got no problem!"

He was absolutely right. *He* did not have any problem; his son had the problem, as was demonstrated when he joined Nat's son at a dealer meeting and proceeded to bend his ear about what an S.O.B. his father was to work with, and how he wished to get a chance to manage the business without his father's nose in every department. He complained that after his father returns from his winter vacation, "he's intolerable the first few days he's back at the dealership, and he changes everything!"

Sound familiar?

Transferring the control and power of a business to a successor can be a very painful, depressing, and anxiety-producing process for the owner. Consequently, family business owners engage in many strategems to avoid facing letting go. The most often-used ploy is the declaration that the successor candidate "is not ready"—even though the successor designate may be fifty years old with twenty-five years' experience in the business.

Another ploy is being "too busy to talk about it." Still another is the "when I was his age" syndrome. This is usually used by family business owners to justify paying their kids less money, or to deify themselves as patron saints for tolerating the modern work habits adopted by their successor candidates. These are the guys who still resent the five-day work week!

There are too many frustrated family business successor candidates whose talents and career potential are being wasted in repressive and tension-laden family business workplaces because of an owner's paranoia about releasing power and control of the business.

On the other hand, countless family business owners have been disappointed and hurt by the failure of their progeny to adequately respond to the challenges of assuming control of their businesses.

Divesting oneself of power and control is extremely difficult. Planning for retirement shouldn't be much different from planning the operation of a business or acquiring additional business. Selecting and training managers to successfully operate the business while you are actively involved may seem different from training successors, but it really isn't. The same rules apply, the big difference being that the rewards for the successorship trainees are much greater and require a higher degree of skill and commitment. Still, planned properly and sincerely, the twilight years of retirement can approach the blissful stereotype.

Making Peace with Retirement

For many people, retirement means a gold watch, a clean break with a thirty- or forty-year-old relationship, and "the time to do the things you always wanted to do."

But retirement is not for everyone! Your typical active, healthy, vibrant older business owner may be scared stiff at the prospect of being put out to pasture. The vision of puttering around the house performing mundane exercises in killing time and stressing out a wife not used to having hubby underfoot can be frightening.

If a capable person elects not to retire and chooses instead to modify work habits by changing the degree of commitment to the job, that person should be encouraged. Life insurance company annals are full of death statistics for people who were forced to retire and give up their reason to live. (Entrepreneurs love to justify their fear of retirement with these statistics.) One of Joe's friends who is now retired liked to say, "Do you know that the life expectancy for a businessman is 3.2 years after retirement?"

Working part-time with the freedom to vacation is ideal. Consulting is another way to remain in the mainstream without the stress of time commitments. But beware: In the context of successorship, this type of "partial retirement" carries with it great hazards to the successor unless there is clear agreement about the role of the owner when he is "in residence."

First, if the successor is given complete authority when Dad is away, then this must hold true when the "old man" is back in town.

Second, if you want your retirement to be partial, be aware that only your time commitment can really be partial. In matters of operational control and authority, there is no such thing as a part-time manager, just as there is no such thing as being partly pregnant. You either are a manager, with all the attendant worries and responsibilities, or you aren't. Successful programs and campaigns in any family business require both short- and long-term planning. These plans require hands-on consistent attention from all managers so subordinates stay enthused and interested in the goals of the plans.

In the dozens of interviews we have conducted with successors, one of the most common complaints is that Dad travels in and out of the business frequently—partially retired—and that each time he comes back, he screws up plans that have been working for months simply by countermanding policies and decisions that have been discussed and agreed upon by the team of managers.

As Robert Townsend notes in his book *Further Up the Organization,* "Please don't underestimate the destructive potential of the retired chief executive who remains on the premises as a 'consultant' or Chairman of the Finance Committee. If you are stuck with a predecessor who has contractual rights to an office and a secretary, insist that he be located someplace else. You can afford to rent him a handsome suite. Otherwise neither you, nor he, nor anyone else will know who's in charge."

No matter how powerful the person, varying degrees of retirement are inevitable. The diminution of physical and mental prowess manifests in all humanity. Time inevitably exacts its price for the years bestowed. There are those rare people for whom nature's process seems forestalled, but these rarities are far outweighed by those who don't know when to let go. There is no sight in the business or sports world as disheartening as a businessman or an athlete attempting to function in a high-powered environment after having "lost his fastball."

Famous entertainers say to "always leave the audience wanting more!" World-class athletes hang it up when they still could eke out another win or two, but not with their accustomed style. This type of attitude is sorely needed in the family business milieu, where too often an aging owner fails to step aside with dignity, empowering the successors, and instead holds on, creating resentment and tension within the business and family.

An intelligently planned-for retirement need not be an end, but an exciting beginning. Townsend writes: "The most successful retirement I ever saw was that of Walter L. Jacobs, founder of the rent-a-car industry and president of Hertz. For five years Walter kept telling everybody he was going to go. He turned authority and responsibility over to his younger people and built personal banking and real estate interests in his selected retirement locale to soak up the energy that might otherwise tempt him to be a pest. When Walter retired neither he nor anyone else went into shock. And the company made new records."

As Dr. Perry Gresham, President Emeritus of Bethany College, West Virginia, writes in his book, *With Wings as Eagles:* "Life is a series of renewals rather than a machine that wears out a little at a time." Dr. Gresham recounts story after story of ordinary people in their seventies and eighties who started successful new careers after the traditional age of retirement. Some famous models are:

- Winston Churchill, who was sixty-six when he became prime minister of Great Britain.

- Benjamin Franklin, who was seventy when the Declaration of Independence was signed in 1776. He was still active in the Constitutional convention when he was in his eighties.
- Ronald Reagan, certainly a prime example of the possibilities of the "twilight years."

Here are some American entrepreneurs who started their business after most people retire:

- Colonel Sanders of Kentucky Fried Chicken opened his first store while in his sixties.
- The legendary Ray Kroc didn't buy into McDonald's until his late fifties.
- Royal Litte, the father of the conglomerate, didn't buy his first business until he was in his fifties; then he bought three hundred more.

A model for planning a fulfilling retirement might look something like this:

- Accept that your life is not eternal and that you are going to die.
- Make a conscious decision that at an appropriate and attainable time, you will change your work habits, sincerely schedule a complete or partial break—and mean it!
- Select and begin to seriously train your successor.
- Think about using your years of knowledge and experience in an ancillary part of your industry. Begin using the personal skills that made your business a success to accomplish this goal while you train your successor.
- Develop and stick to a regular program of physical fitness.
- Make time for personal pursuits. These could be careers you would have chosen, had timing and opportunities been different.
- Investigate the innovative new educational oppportunities available for mature adults. (Nat received his master's degree in Education from Cambridge College when he was sixty-two.)
- Readopt the "What do I want to be when I grow up?" attitude you had as an aspiring youth. Simply modify it to "What do I want to do when I change careers?"—if a new career is what you want.
- Begin to realize that others can run your business successfully without you.

You may have felt indispensable during your tenure, but others may actually have had equal or even better talent and commitment. Let them offer it now. But, if the aforementioned model is not acceptable, there are other options. You can:

- Live and work forever.
- Create havoc when you die because you thought you were immortal and didn't designate and train a successor.
- Become a royal pain in the ass to your family and aspiring progeny because you won't let go of control and power.
- Play lousy golf because you never practiced.
- Die prematurely because you didn't plan and look forward to a meaningful and fulfilling retirement.

Partnership Pitfalls

When partners own equal shares of a family business, and each owner has a child who is a potential succeeding chief executive, conflicts are inevitable.

Realizing they might not agree on this issue is the first step partners must take toward solving it. The successorship issue must be addressed early, and unemotionally (easier said than done, I know). The primary issue to be addressed is the relationship between the prospective successors. The partner/owners must realize that, unlike them, their children have not shared the creation of the business and the attendant bonding. The owners cannot expect their sons and daughters to feel anything like that kind of kinship for each other. This issue must be addressed—with the help of an unbiased third party (consultant or other outside adviser), if necessary. The earlier this process is begun, the better the chances of avoiding destructive conflicts between the progeny should a partner die prematurely or become disabled.

Ideally, the partners should choose the most qualified person from among all the willing children to be CEO and distribute assets in a way that will not affect the day-to-day operation of the business by that person. Good financial returns generated by a competent CEO from a well-run business will salve most bruised egos.

If, however, an unresolvable successorship conflict arises, both families would be best served by an equitable buyout. Even if the more qualified successor belongs to the family being bought out, it is better to liquidate the business and save the money than to have an ugly dispute that destroys the value of the business.

Admittedly, there are many variations on partnerships. The partner with a greater percentage stake in the business will be able to push his or her child as successor more successfully. If the most qualified successor candidate belongs to the junior family, though, and a satisfactory deal for his participation cannot be negotiated, he should resign and start his own business. There is no one more miserable than a talented partner who must spend his prime years subservient to an incompetent CEO. Unfortunately, the wrong Golden Rule is often applied: "He who has the gold makes the rules."

Just as ownership is shared in a partnership, so are the challenges of successorship. Unless the partners make a serious and sustained effort to make it happen, the sheer complexity of human emotion among potential successors jockeying for position will probably make the passing on of the business impossible. The presence of a nonfamily owner may provide a qualified family successor candidate with a mentor who could ease communication, though. Even a partner with no children available for or interested in successorship should share the burden of the process with his or her partner.

R_x FOR POTENTIAL SUCCESSORSHIP HEADACHES

FOR THE SUCCESSOR CANDIDATE

1. Make a serious time commitment to working in the family business.
2. Don't think a career in the family business is your birthright.
3. Research and consider stewardship in a similar nonfamily-owned business.
4. Be empathetic to the parent/owner's problems with letting go of the reins of the business.
5. Reject unrealistic expectations and assumptions resulting from poor communication between family members.
6. Be prepared for possible hostility and resentment from long-term employees during your early years in the business.
7. Don't overlook special personal talents out of a sense of obligation to perpetuate the family business.

FOR THE PARENT/OWNER

1. Don't become obsessed with being "fair" in handing out management positions to family members. Simply because one qualified sibling earns a key management position does not dictate that other, less qualified family members be equally recognized.
2. Be cognizant of female family members who demonstrate an interest in careers in the family business.
3. Allow in-laws who hold positions in the family business to grow in their jobs based on talent and performance rather than the quality of their marriages to family members.

4. Do not deceive successor candidates with fictitious plans for your retirement. If you honestly don't believe you can retire, share this information with family members. This will go a long way toward eliminating invalid expectations that have the potential to create stress in the business.

   Retirement is not for everyone! If your successor family members understand that you expect to work until death or disability, then they can plan their own lives accordingly. You'll be surprised how understanding and tolerant successor candidates can be about this issue if it is openly discussed.

7. Making the Many Transitions

The First Transition: From Entrepreneur to Manager

Ironically, the family business owner who starts out trying to realize his impossible dream and succeeds then faces what we call the Impossible Transition. Much of this book has dealt with successorship issues, but before that point is reached, the parent/owner must cross this impossible bridge. He must learn to change from a creator and originator into an administrator or let go enough to hire some good administrators.

When Joe Mancuso founded the Center for Entrepreneurial Management (CEM) in Worcester, Massachusetts, in 1978, he created two slogans for it. CEM Inc. is a unique information middleman, supplying help to growing businesses. Joe wanted to have an association that would allow entrepreneurs to share ideas and benefit from common wisdom, and CEM has become that by building on these two slogans:

- It's OK to be independent, but there is no reason to be alone.
- The professional manager protects resources, but the entrepreneurial manager creates them.

This second slogan captures the difficulty inherent in the transition from entrepreneur to manager.

It is very rare for someone to be both an originator and an administrator. The experience of a bachelor friend presently on his third business dramatizes the difficulty of this transition.

In the mid-sixties, along with a college roommate, he started his first small electronics company. The two built the company from the initial $3,000 investment to a modest size and then sold it for about $100,000 to a major electronics corporation. It was a typical first entrepreneurial venture with the attendant management mistakes, not a big success or a big failure.

They invested the $100,000 in a new company and again worked hard and long, only this time they hit a winning market with a winning product and made it big. Our bachelor friend soon found his talents were not matched to the task of running a $10-million company. The two partners wisely agreed to hire an outside administrator to assume the presidency and run the company, thereby avoiding a management mistake that could have brought the house down.

Having made it past the Impossible Transition, our friend found himself to be a good-looking bachelor in his thirties with several million dollars in cash. Many people in his shoes would have lounged the rest of their lives away somewhere in the Caribbean, but, don't forget, our friend was an entrepreneur. He was miserable leading a purposeless life. The moral is that the Impossible Transition can be a shocker even if you do get through it. Prepare for it by talking with others who have survived the process. They can help you just as recovered alcoholics help new AA members.

Based upon ten three-day CEO Club programs attended by over 200 CEOs in a six-year period, we've been able to develop certain rules that seem to apply to the job of CEO and to CEO transitions. For instance, in businesses between $1 and $100 million, the CEO's performance is often the single most crucial element in the enterprise's success. And, while the transition from entrepreneurial manager to administrator occurs at different stages and sizes depending on the business, we found that generally the $20 to $40 million annual sales range is the most common time for this transition.

The belief that the entrepreneur is most effective in the early stages of a growing business, whereas the professional manager is preferred once the business becomes established, is widely accepted, but few know how and when to execute this all-important transition. Family business owners may recognize the need for long-range planning and budgeting, but their effectiveness at creating such plans is inversely proportional to their need for them.

Organizational charts for entrepreneurially managed companies tend to look like the air-traffic controller's chart for O'Hare airport—fifty-six people reporting directly to the owner.

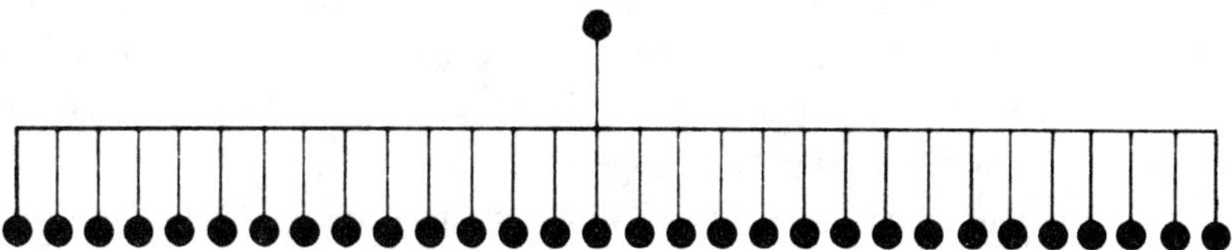

The professionally managed company has layers of management, and no more than seven people report to any single manager. It looks like this, but everyone wonders, "Who is supposed to decide what?"

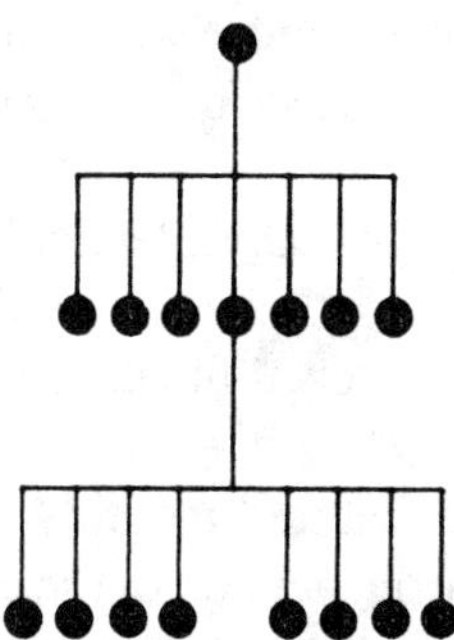

Neither the entrepreneurial nor the professional management style is inherently good or bad; instead, each is good or bad depending on the needs of the individual company—and those needs vary at different stages of growth. Here are some basic pluses and minuses of each style:

Entrepreneurial

Minus	*Plus*
People in the dark	Fun
Unmotivated people	Quick decisions
Driving people crazy	Not a quitter
No planning (formal)	Vision/Dream
Frightening to money types	

Professional

Minus	*Plus*
Slow decisions	Consistency
No fun	Ability to implement resources
Tolerates mistakes	Growth opportunities for people
Politics/games	Process
Loses closeness to market	

All too often, the founder of a small business is kicked out of the business in order to save it. This occurs so often that the transition from entrepreneur to professional manager sometimes seems impossible. That's why so many businesses are sold at this stage.

The story of Apple Computers is typical. Steven Jobs and Steve Wozniak founded the business and created wealth for hundreds of people. Wozniak left first, to pursue a career as a rock music promoter and then to found another business called Cloud 9. Wozniak sold that one and is looking to start another. Jobs was eventually fired from Apple by the "professional" president, John Scully (Jobs was one of those who selected him), who had come to Apple after a successful tenure at PepsiCo. Jobs went on to form a business named, appropriately, NeXT, Inc.

The pattern was virtually identical for Nolan Bushnell, who founded Atari, Catalyst Technologies, Pizza-Time Theatre, and at least a dozen other businesses. After each reached the critical stage, Bushnell was removed in favor of the Professionals.

Such stories are featured monthly in both *Inc.* and *Success* magazines. They are the entrepreneurial version of the continuing soap opera. The dream of many U.S. entrepreneurs is to do it all over again despite age or other obstacles. They like the "doing" of creating a business better than the maintenance of it. Where does this leave the entrepreneurial owner of a family business, who has an added incentive to "maintain" but may not feel suited to that managerial role?

The first step might be to acknowledge that such an owner will have to wear two different hats—those of "entrepreneurial manager" and of "professional manager"—and work to be good at each role. There is no reason why an entrepreneur cannot also be a professional manager.

As Frederick Smith, the founder of Federal Express, said in addressing the New York chapter of the CEO Club, "Just because I spotted a market niche for overnight package delivery is no reason I can't also run a billion-dollar business. It's like speaking a foreign language and running. *They are neither related nor mutually exclusive.*"

At Joe's CEO Club management seminars, each participant is given a chance to cherry-pick the best aspects of the two management styles presented. The best of both styles should then be integrated into the participant's own style, allowing him or her to build upon existing styles and skills. Awareness of the need to incorporate both of these management styles into your family business is half the battle.

ENTREPRENEURIAL MANAGER: Ready! Fire! Aim!
PROFESSIONAL MANAGER: Ready! Ready! Aim!

Here are a dozen specific notions that came out of our seminars, which both the entrepreneurial and the professional manager feel are central to the task of being a CEO:

1. Picking good people is the essence of a CEO's job.
2. CEOs never fire someone soon enough.
3. A company's weakest vice-president often shares the CEO's area of expertise; i.e., a CEO with a particular expertise is reluctant to allow others to play in his sandbox, so he hires a weak V.P. in order to justify spending a little time back in the sandbox supporting that person.
4. The mission statement of a CEO for the business is the single most tangible measure of the CEO's effectiveness.
5. Avoid the neutron bomb syndrome—where the buildings and equipment are all standing but the people are all gone. A CEO should open the door and count to three before entering a room.
6. Avoid the mushroom theory of management—where you keep everyone in the dark and throw a lot of manure on them.
7. A leader with both entrepreneurial and professional skills inspires people to have confidence in themselves, not just in the leader.
8. Boards of outside directors and advisers are mandatory.
9. A plan's effectiveness is a multiplication of the plan's value times its general acceptance by the group charged with implementing it. The formula is: Value times Commitment equals Effectiveness.
10. A CEO on his deathbed seldom wishes he had spent more time at the office.
11. Every person in the perfect organization can say: I know what I'm supposed to accomplish and by when.
12. Negative motivation programs should be considered as part of an overall motivation program for the business.

THE SECOND TRANSITION: SUCCESSORSHIP

Why do business owners want to navigate the turbulent waters of successorship, anyway? What's in it for them? After all, the simplest solution would be to sell a successful business to a qualified buyer and use the proceeds to secure the owner's future and still have enough left to bequeath to heirs.

Nearly every entrepreneur whose company reaches maturity eventually faces the decision to encourage or discourage his or her children to join the family business. The best way to discover latent attitudes about retirement and transition held by family business members is to start exploring them early. Each case is different, but this generalization very often applies: *When a child joins the business, he or she does so prematurely and for the wrong reasons!*

Whenever possible, children should start their careers elsewhere to broaden their experience. This gives them a fresh perspective and new ideas and experience they can bring into the family business later. Most important, they enter the family business with a solid level of confidence gained outside the protective confines of the family. Not only will they be better-qualified successor candidates, they will have the confidence and experience to cope with the inherent challenges of successorship. So please don't prematurely push your offspring into the family business. Let them know that if they want it, it's there, but not as an easy ride through life. Make them work. You did, and it did you a world of good. It's tough enough to be born with a silver spoon, let alone succeed with a silver foot in your mouth.

Business owners decide to keep the business in the family for a wide variety of good and not-so-good reasons, both emotional and financial. To prevent the transition to the next generation from being not-so-good or even traumatic, though, several crucial issues must be addressed:

- Business owners must address the finiteness of their lives by legally planning the distribution of their worldly assets when they die. This is more than complicated enough for any person with an abundance of worldly goods, but for family business owners also trying to balance the potential desires of their children to join the business, it can be a nightmare. There are often frustrating encounters with tax laws once an owner decides to pass on company stock to a worthy successor, for example, or serious cash flow implications to be faced. Good professional advice becomes mandatory, and must be retained early in the process. Later, you'll see how this issue crippled the Binghams of Louisville.
- Parent/owners need to become coaches and teachers, a role that may be very difficult for high-powered, successful entrepreneurs to assume. Objective selection and proper coaching of the next-generation CEO is vital if the successor candidate is going to be equipped to handle the transition. The annals of family business history are full of tales of CEO transitions that failed because the parent/owner was a great doer, but a terrible coach and teacher. The principle of "those who can, do, and those who can't, teach" is demonstrated clearly in professional sports. More often than not, great sports stars have become below-average coaches and managers. Ted Williams was one of the greatest hitters in baseball, yet his short career as manager of the Washington Senators was poor. Pete Rose had more base hits than any player in major-league history, yet he couldn't handle the personal

discipline required to be a successful manager. The legendary quarterback Bart Starr of Green Bay was better on the field than off. Very few superstars have the ability to recognize potential ability in their players and inspire them to reach for it.

Conversely, some of the greatest and most successful coaches and managers, such as Casey Stengel (Brooklyn Dodgers and New York Yankees), Joe McCarthy (New York Yankees and Boston Red Sox), and Vince Lombardi (Green Bay Packers) had lukewarm success as players in their fields. But they had the ability to not only recognize talent and potential but to empower their players to aspire to levels beyond what they thought they could reach. The most successful entrepreneurs recognize their managerial limitations early and hire others to fill the gaps, allowing the entrepreneur to do what he or she does best. Just look at Ed Land's career at Polaroid. Although he founded the company, he preferred the title of chief scientist to president. In the case of training the kids, this is where the trusted lieutenant or mentor can come in handy.

- Parent/owners should recognize and separate their personal power and control traits from the transition process. It is difficult for a successful entrepreneur, who has been accustomed to being impatient with failure in his people, to suddenly shift gears when it comes to his son or daughter and become the teacher who knows that life's most important lessons are often learned through failures. The personal discipline required to allow fledglings to temporarily fail in order to learn is generally absent from parents who shelter their kids from adversity, as well as from the entrepreneur to whom failure is anathema. The combination of protective parent and successful entrepreneur can cause serious transition problems. To some extent, this is a primary reason for the pattern we often see of strong, weak, strong, weak over the generations.
- Loving, caring family business owners should not be afraid to give some thought to what is best for them and their spouses—not just their children—during the twilight years of their lives. Lots of kids are insensitive to the emotional turmoil parents face during this period of transition. Their lifelong pictures of their high-energy, successful parent's career in the business may not be consistent with where the parent is currently or wants to be. The transition players should frequently share career expectations and visions for the future of the business in order to eliminate misguided assumptions and invalid expectations—two common pitfalls of CEO transition in family business.
- Strong emotional forces attack family business owners just prior to and during the successorship process. Owners and successors should be aware

of these forces. For example, perpetuating their life creation through talented heirs may help to alleviate some of their sense of finality. The successorship process can then assume an agenda similar to the feudal lord's or king's, whose major concern is the continuity of the blood lines. Then there is the "Joe who?" syndrome that strikes when an owner finds many of the favorite status symbols he earned throughout his life becoming extinct. Fear of no longer being recognized at the workplace or in the industrial community, of becoming "Joe who?" can overwhelm an owner.

- The kids' attitudes must be considered. Upon examination, business owners may find their children consider the family business their birthright. Some are capable of succeeding in the business, but others are simply looking to ride the family gravy train.
- A spouse may put so much pressure on an owner to let an obviously unqualified child into the business that the owner gives in, causing irreparable damage to both the business and the offspring. Family business owners must make it clear to all family members that decisions are not based only on parental love and consideration for the child, but also on the owner's years of experience with personnel decisions and, most importantly, on what's best for the business.

  On the other hand, high-powered parent/owners tend to develop career expectations for their progeny, often with minimal input from the children about what *they* want. Powerful entrepreneurs have the ability to intimidate and coerce loving family members into careers in the family business. Family members who are being pushed toward a career they don't want must assert themselves, even at the risk of seriously disappointing parents they love. Courageous communication is imperative early in the game. In a high-tech business, for example, sons and daughters who wanted to be considered successors might have to make educational commitments as early as high school. What worked for the founder when at "that age" may be inappropriate and unrealistic for his or her children.

An aspiring successor should ask himself several important questions when confronted with the potential responsibility of becoming the CEO of the family business:

- Is this the career I would have chosen, if I had had a choice?
- If I don't accept the challenge of successorship, will I be sacrificing my birthright?
- Is my alternative to a career in the family business important enough to give up the perks I've seen this family enjoy from the business?

- Is this an opportunity for me, or an obligation?
- If I don't accept, will the position be given to someone who will not acknowledge that I am entitled to my share of the family assets?
- Do I have the courage to confront, and perhaps seriously disappoint, a parent I love and respect a great deal?

A valuable exercise for a family business owner would be to imagine a purely professional team of managers taking over the operation of the family business. Would the pros be content with the current managers as well as the managers-in-training? Often, the dynamics of the family overwhelm business decisions and place incompetent family members prematurely in key management positions. Such a family member is usually protected from accountability during the life of the parent/owner, and is firmly entrenched by the time a crisis hits the business after the parent's death. A professional management company, free of emotional attachments to the family members, would not allow this to happen.

A Third Possible Transition: Alternatives to the Firstborn Son

Fortunately, the successor candidate field has expanded significantly in recent years. Time was, the oldest son was automatically nominated to succeed his father as CEO. Younger and female siblings were automatically excluded from the successorship process. Talent was not a major consideration, even though in many cases, the oldest brother only got older, while the younger brother and his sisters got smarter. Just see the Binghams' story in chapter 8.

As reported in our chapter on women in the family business (chapter 4), daughters and wives have become excellent candidates for leadership of the family business. It is no longer automatic for the eldest son to succeed his father in the business. Talent and commitment, not age or sex, are now the benchmarks. In Nat Shulman's case, his youngest son is the CEO and his daughter is in line to assume CEO status in a subsidiary company. His oldest son, meanwhile, is very happy in an entirely different business.

With all these additional options for successor candidates, it is no longer obligatory for the eldest son to sacrifice his future and desires to the requirements of the family business. On the other hand, because of all these new choices, a less-than-talented heir-apparent cannot assume he will take over the family business. He will have to compete for the job with brothers and sisters.

An article titled "Historian Links Birth Order to Innovation" by Daniel Goleman appeared in the Science section of the *New York Times* on Tuesday, May 8, 1990. In the piece, Frank Sulloway, a science historian, states that firstborns are more likely to accept prevailing views and parental standards. The later children are the ones to rebel and upset the applecart. In 1988 and 1989, there were forty-five scientific reports on birth order, and more than one-third found it to have no effect, but Dr. Sulloway claims that firstborns are more likely to defend current theories (especially scientific ones) and later-born children are more likely to attack them.

Over a dozen years, Joe has surveyed the 3,000 dues-paying members of the Center for Entrepreneurial Management. His data, which we report in appendix I, indicate that two-thirds of his membership are firstborn children. Because the family size of this group averages three children, the norm should be one-third oldest children rather than the two-thirds actually observed. This indicates that entrepreneurs—who, as a group, are innovative and even somewhat rebellious—may actually tend to be firstborn children, contradicting Dr. Sulloway's picture of the conservative firstborn child.

Nonfamily members who hold high management positions in the family business should also be seriously considered for CEO positions. If there is no qualified family member, selecting a talented manager to buy out the company over time may best serve the long-term interests of family members and the business. There are many ways to arrange that such a buyout require a reasonable investment (which may be financed by the family) from the manager and a long-term buyout from future profits *only.* The profits-only buyout ensures that the business will stay with the person the owner selects to perpetuate it for a reasonable time.

To make such deals, retain the best legal and financial talent available. Seek specialists in the sale of businesses. If family lawyers and accountants are not capable of handling the details of such a transaction, they should be used only as advisers to the specialists. We've seen too many deals consummated by well-meaning family attorneys and accountants in which important issues such as the inflation of real estate were overlooked. In some of these cases, options to buy the real estate at a predesignated price became the most valuable part of the transaction for the purchaser, at a heavy loss of potential revenue for the sellers.

Start the Successorship Process Early

Training a competent successor candidate while the business owner is healthy and available allows everyone plenty of time to discover comfortable new identities.

First and foremost, an owner must never deceive family members with promises of his retirement when he doesn't intend to quit. If family members are going to have to wait until death or infirmity claims him to assume leadership, then he must let it be known. There are many bright entrepreneurs who refuse to acknowledge that their lives and careers are finite and will never retire. That's OK. However, such parent/owners must not delude successor candidates about their prospects (nil) for taking over the reins during the owner's lifetime. Remember, Armand Hammer of Occidental Petroleum stayed at the helm until his nineties.

While playing this cat-and-mouse game with the fortunes of their successor candidates, owners sometimes massage the situation by declaring the candidate "not ready." This type of owner will never let go, for he really has no other interest in life. Until illness, disability, or death comes on the scene, the successor candidate of such an owner should resign himself to his heir-apparent status . . . or resign.

Being wise enough to allow the competent successor to discover an identity in the business by avoiding debilitating and regressive interference will allow the senior generation to share in the glow of their progeny's accomplishments in the business they created. Nat's son, for example, requested that Nat stop coming to regular staff meetings because he could not function effectively as the meeting leader if his father was present. Nat was hurt by the exclusion, but luckily was able to remember how almost forty years ago his older brother had placed him in the same position.

Being wise enough to let go, secure in the knowledge that the business will be properly passed on, senior members can move to other interests they may have wanted to pursue all their lives. Nat, for example, went back to college and became a writer.

Likewise, it behooves competent successors to be sensitive to the feelings of the older generation. It is tempting for successors to overreact to alleged meddling by the owner in the operation of the business. Often, this is the result of the successor's lack of confidence and security—they forget to treat their benefactors with the heavy doses of kindness and empathy needed to make this all-important transition.

Many dynamic successors have zero tolerance for the feelings of the senior members. The successors feel tremendous pressure to prove how well they can run the business and don't have time for emotional issues. One son, in fact, reportedly had his father forcibly removed from the business premises by the police. It's not so uncommon.

A few years ago, Joe Mancuso and his family toured one of the wonders of the world, the Taj Mahal. Not the one in Atlantic City owned by Donald Trump, but the edifice outside the city of Agra, a few hours north of Delhi, the capital of India. Built on the banks of the Jamuna River, this perfectly symmetrical building is perhaps India's most beautiful monument. This is said to be the biggest single tourist attraction in the world, one of the Seven Wonders, a tribute of one man's undying love for his wife.

Built amidst landscaped gardens, this bejeweled white marble building was erected as the final resting place for Mumtaz Mahal, the wife of the Mughal Emperor, Shah Jehan. She died unexpectedly in childbirth while in her thirties. Begun in 1630, it took twenty-two years to complete, at great cost in labor and money.

The tragedy of this story is what happened to this father/emperor in his later years. Shah Jehan had wanted to erect a duplicate monument in black marble as his final resting place, but was overthrown by his son Aurangzeb before he could undertake this task. Shah Jehan spent the last sixteen years of his life a prisoner in his palace at Agra, from which he could view the Taj Mahal. Aurangzeb did erect a tomb for his father within the Taj Mahal next to that of Mumtaz. It was one of the few acts of kindness the son showed to his father after overthrowing him and seizing the Mughal empire for himself.

The story of a son overthrowing a father to seize control of an empire repeats itself in many cultures. The story of the Taj Mahal is probably the single most often told tale of succession in the world. The king is dead. Long live the king.

Wise successors will realize emotional issues can bring down the house if not addressed, and will take advantage of the opportunity to repay the many times they were comforted by their parents.

It would serve all family business members well to constantly remember that the successorship process would never have begun without the sanction of the parent/owner. He or she could have simply sold the business and pocketed the proceeds, but chose instead the more difficult route with its accompanying stresses in order to keep the business in the family.

8. Famous Family Business Lessons

We wrestled with making this the first chapter, because it is more lesson-prone than any other, but we concluded it could be off-putting to start a book with examples of how *not* to run a family business. So, we chose the more traditional approach of moving from the general to the specific. If you think we are restating the obvious when we talk about boards of advisers, or about women's roles or about successors, try reading this chapter and then go back to the ones that you skimmed over the first time. It will do you a world of good, and it will make our advice look *real* good.

As we were writing this book, the entrepreneurial heroes of the eighties, Donald and Ivana Trump, were carrying on in their ongoing soap opera—which ran in the *New York Post* for months—"Trump: The Divorce." How all this hoopla will have affected them nobody knows, but we believe the principles we advocate in this book would help them as surely as they can help your family (which at times may not seem any more sane than the Trumps!). The lessons of the Henry Ford or Seward Johnson stories most likely apply to the Trumps, too.

The creation of an empire requires motivation and commitment bordering on obsession. Just read the entrepreneurial characteristics in appendix I. These folks are not always nice people. It's damn hard to like Donald Trump, perhaps even for his kids. We're not just picking on the Donald, either. The same goes for Steven Jobs, in his thirties and still single, and for cable king Ted Turner. Still, almost everyone admires what these people have accomplished, and the same goes for a monstrous father like Henry Ford.

Strong fathers seem to have sons at one end or the other of the spectrum from weak to strong, but never in the middle. Trump, Fred Smith of Federal Express, and Howard Hughes were all the offspring of very strong fathers. The legendary insurance great, W. Clement Stone, on the other hand, outlived both his children, neither of whom could follow in his footsteps, and J. Paul Getty's oldest son, once the world's wealthiest man, scorned all business pursuits for a quiet career as an artist.

For the story of Henry Ford's domination of his son, see the section on the Fords in this chapter. H. L. Hunt's children by his first marriage squandered a fortune worth billions of dollars. His children by his second and third marriages did much better with the family fortune and business, bringing to mind a comment we once heard Herb Cohen of the Power Negotiation Institute of Chicago make: "Kids are like pancakes—it's best to throw out the first batch."

Entrepreneurial families tend to follow a pattern of strong, weak, strong, weak through the generations. This pattern holds true for the Johnson family. We suspect we'll begin to see the same pattern with entrepreneurial mothers and daughters. It'll be fascinating to see what happens to Donald Trump's children after two generations of strong fathers.

The histories of some of the most famous family businesses in the world are more instructive as examples of how not to have a successful family business. The family businesses we discuss in this chapter share one common problem: success of the business at the *expense* of the family. And, in the Bingham case, for example, the family disintegration during the buildup of the business becomes the eventual downfall of the business. A family business cannot be deemed truly successful unless both the goals of the business and the family—which, as we've pointed out through this book, are often diametrically opposed—are met.

In this chapter, we have chosen to encapsulate some famous stories from the annals of family business. After reading all our platitudes in the preceding chapters, we thought real stories, with human blemishes, were needed to spur you to action. By examining these famous family business lessons, you can perhaps learn how to avoid the problems they illustrate. All are true stories, as in family business the truth is always wilder than fiction.

FAMILY BUSINESS CASE HISTORY

Stew Leonard's World's Largest Dairy Store

Stew Leonard was a second-generation milkman with a home delivery route until 1968, when Connecticut state highway construction forced him to relocate his dairy plant. With the help of a loan from the Small Business Administration, he built a unique store around a glass-enclosed dairy plant in Norwalk, Connecticut. Twenty-six additions to the original building later, the 106,000-square-foot complex sprawls on eight and a half acres.

Current sales are approaching $100 million at the location in Norwalk alone. An additional store has been opened in Danbury under the direction of son Tom, and other locations are in process. Stew Leonard's was featured in Tom Peters' bestseller *A Passion for Excellence* as one of the best-run companies in America. The store has a country fair atmosphere, with employees dressed as farm animals strolling the aisles to amuse customers, prompting the *New York Times*, *New York Magazine*, and *Fortune* to refer to Stew Leonard's as a "Disneyland Dairy Store." There are also cows that moo when a child presses a button, two eight-foot dogs who play the banjo and serenade shoppers with country tunes, and a farmer who sings and talks to passing children.

The company is a partnership between Leonard and his wife, Marianne. The eldest son, Stew, Jr., is president of the company. Younger son, Tom, and daughters Beth and Jill, as well as two of Leonard's sisters, two brothers-in-law, and various other relatives also are part of the team. The Leonards are so convinced of the value of families working together that 55 percent of the six hundred people working at the store have at least one relative who also works there.

Stew Leonard, Sr., passed the ball to the next generation several years ago. In addition to his namesake being president of the company, son Tom is solely in charge of the Danbury store (150 employees), daughter Jill is manager of personnel, and daughter Beth manages the store bakery (aptly called Bethy's Bakery). According to the Food Marketing Institute, this bakery annually sells more than twenty times as much as any other in-store bakery in America.

Stew Leonard, Jr., recounts the following story about his father's near-obsession with family in business: "One time we were all sitting around the dinner table and my father took out four sticks bound together. He set them on the table and asked, 'Who can break these?'

"Beth and Jill started first and Tommy and I said, 'Ah, that'll be no sweat.' We tried to do it but we couldn't break the bound sticks, and handed them back to our father. He then undid the binding holding the sticks together and handed each of us a single stick, saying, 'Now try it.' And each one of them snapped easily—but together, they couldn't be broken!"

Stew Leonard, Sr., says, "When there are children in the business, there is tremendous loyalty and trust and dependability and feeling of ownership and caring. The disadvantage is that it is very hard to wear two hats as a boss and as a parent."

A manifestation of the "two-hats syndrome" happened several years ago with Leonard's younger son, Tom. Tom, then a recent college graduate, wanted time off to drive to Fort Lauderdale for a concert. The boss (Hat 1, Dad) said no. Tom went anyway. On his arrival home, the boss (Hat 2) told his employee he was fired. Dad then asked his son how he could help him find a job.

Leonard, Sr., whose father died at age fifty-seven, shares: "When you're young and you're taking over the family business, there's not a day that goes by that you don't wish you could talk to your dad and wish you could ask him to explain something.

"Don't live your life as though you have 2,000 years before you. That's been our philosophy in our business. My son was made president of Stew Leonard's three years ago. I was only fifty-five years old. The business was growing and it needed me. But I think that's one of the real challenges for the founder, to hand the baton over, to hand the power to others. There's a little ego involved. You have to adjust to it, you have to see them make mistakes and just bite your bottom lip. But most of all, you need to be a coach and a back-patter.

"Also, business can be fun! This is the mainstay of our business from the customer through the team member, to the family member: Business should be fun! What we're trying to do is make an experience, especially with our own children here, that success in our line is becoming yourself at your very best. It's got nothing to do with money. It's how you are going to develop. And I always say that if one of our children wanted to become a rock star, Marianne and I would have gladly bought the guitar."

How Do the Leonards Resolve Family Issues and Problems?

STEW, SR. We try to departmentalize our business. Beth runs Bethy's Bakery, and she is the undisputed boss. That's her domain and the other kids have nothing to say about the way she runs it. The same is true for Jill, who runs Personnel and Human Services, and for Tom in the Danbury store. We don't stick our noses in their departments. We let them run their areas and we judge them by results. And we're not day-to-day people, we're "let's see the bottom line, what-the-results-are" people. And the bottom line does not necessarily mean profit, it means, what are the results? Our philosophy has always been, let's build something great and the profits will take care of themselves. We're not profit-oriented, and we're not financially oriented. We realize that both are important; however, we happen to be more happy-customer-oriented.

STEW, JR. We've tried a lot of things. One thing we try to do is ask how serious is the problem, and then if it's something we can work out together, we usually try to do that over lunch or dinner with the person. If that doesn't work, sometimes we'll get the kids together. All of us will sit down and try to hash it out. And if that doesn't work, we bring in a gavel with Dad and Mom sitting in. It has been suggested by John Ward, our consultant, that we develop a board of directors to help resolve business and family decisions.

How Do You Assess Each Family Member's Performance—Their Contribution to the Numbers?

STEW, SR. It's not a competitive thing to see how well Beth does—better than Danbury or what-not. We don't compete among ourselves that way. There's no competition between the four children. We're in it together, it's a team effort and the results are the whole company.

How Do You Extend the Idea of Family and the Idea of Opportunity to Nonfamily Members in the Organization?

STEW, JR. That really gets to the question of evaluating performances. As far as the family goes, we really are performance-oriented. There's always been that philosophy that if you can't measure it, you can't manage it. And we really try to measure a lot of stuff. Even the cleanliness of our building is measured. Employee attitudes get measured. The performance of groups of people within each of our departments get measured. When you come into the store, it's like the family doesn't really exist anymore. It's a performance thing. The boss of our store is the customer and that's something that everybody is working at. We really go to great lengths with our other managers and people at the store to make sure they see that what gets rewarded at the store is performance. We have people who had started in high school and are making $50,000 to $60,000 after being here about ten years. Other people who have done a great job are up around $100,000. We reward everybody real well and believe in paying for performance.

STEW, SR. The point is what gets rewarded gets repeated. Over 55 percent of our team members have a family member also working in our business. And we are literally a big happy business, a big happy family, with half our staff having a relative or family member working there. So we have to have pretty definite rules about how that's run. And one of the things we try is to keep them out of each other's hair. That is, the family member isn't working directly with his or her husband or wife. But we find it a great advantage in one respect, because the business is carried home afterward. The other thing we find is that, if the mother recommended her daughter to come and become a cashier, the daughter comes and she not only has me for a boss, she also has her mother.

TOM. Opportunity is even greater at Stew Leonard's because there are family members spread throughout the organization. People who are doing a great job are recognized much faster than if there was just one person who was responsible for all the promotions.

How Do You Handle the Succession Process from the Father to the Next Generation? How Do You Divide up Responsibilities?

STEW, JR. One thing is that my father really has tried to relinquish a lot of day-to-day control. He's more of a teacher. I know the hardest part about succession, personally, is that it's one thing to give me the title of president but nothing changes the day after. You have to earn respect from those other people, and that takes years sometimes. My father has had some very loyal, great people who built that whole thing up with him. And you can't have a junior or a Leonard or someone else walking in and expect those people to suddenly take orders from him. Once they gain respect for you, then the succession process is a little bit easier.

STEW, SR. We're great believers in Dale Carnegie and we've sent over 1,000 people, including all of our family, through Dale Carnegie several times, because I think it's an ongoing learning process to be diplomatic about the successorship problem. And it is a problem. We have an older relative, Marianne's brother, who has been with me since I started the business. He's a vice-president, and he's not going to be president. He didn't like it but he knew it. And there was the day that I had to say to him that I decided to make Stew, Jr., the president, and he didn't like to hear that. He has adjusted to it—he doesn't have a choice in that. This isn't a town meeting, it's a family business and somebody has to run it. And you don't help the thing by delaying it. There's a time when that's one of the jobs a father has is to say, "OK, you're going to run the business." If you can make it smooth, and make it so that the son earns his stripes, it might even be a better company with him. That's what you're after.

John Ward is director of the family business program at Loyola University in Chicago. He is one of the foremost respected family business consultants in the world, and has consulted with the Stew Leonard family for several years. Here are some Leonard family observations by John Ward:

- Stew Leonard, Sr., gives tremendous credit and appreciation for the contribution of his wife, Marianne. She accepted primary responsibility for rearing the children well and giving her husband a positive, supportive environment.
- Stew Leonard is not money-driven. Instead, he is driven by personal philosophies and by the challenges of management.
- Leonard, Sr., made a commitment to succession planning and attended to it at a very young age. Stew, Jr., is already president of a $100-million business at the age of thirty-two. The future disposition of the company stock has been determined; stock will be split in four equal ways among the offspring. Stew, Sr., realizes that while the communication and implementation of succession are not flawless, these flaws are best overcome with extra time and extra parental attention, while the parents are still the active family leaders and while the children's career paths and self-concepts are not totally rigid.
- While Stew, Jr., enjoys the title and privilege of president, his brother, brother-in-law, and sisters, all of whom work in the business, understand and empathize with the serious responsibility held by Stew, Jr. They don't see it as merely a matter of privilege and perks.
- Stew, Sr., has developed and pursues many new passions and activities—feeling that these new exciting ideas are actually competing with his time at the store. This makes letting go that much easier and feasible.

This is a family and a business whose values are extremely important. They are reinforced daily—in business and in the family. Many of the same values drive both the business and family life. Most importantly, the values among the four siblings are very homogeneous and assumed by all to be so. In short, the family and business value systems are powerful, congruent, homogeneous, and substantially overlapping.

There are three stages of family business evolution: Stage one, the entrepreneurial or parent stage; stage two, the family or sibling partnership stage; and stage three, the dynasty or cousins-in-business-together stage. The toughest stage is number two. (This is where the Leonards are.)

In the second stage, most of the issues in family business concern fairness and equity. It's during stage two that some very clear philosophies must be developed about "what's mine, what's yours, and what's theirs?" For example:

- Who benefits, and how much, from the growth of the business?
- How to pay, offer benefits, perks, and time off?
- How much do we share personal investment opportunities with each other—at least on a first right-of-refusal basis?
- How much do we share outside business interests and learning opportunities?
- How much do we share in the burdens of bad fortune or bad health that might strike one of us?
- How much do we share the benefits and wealth of the business with key nonfamily employees—such as stock for senior executives?

At this stage of development (stage two), the family business is better off adopting a family-first, not a business-first, approach to these questions. The business is no stronger than the partner relationship among equal sibling shareholders.

The next philosophical question is how to reconcile two competing, deeply felt values; the devotion to individual, entrepreneurial drive and freedom versus the desire for a cooperative family team. This issue will influence several topics, among them the following:

- Future equity distribution—especially in new ventures.
- Opportunities provided under particular terms for future family members.
- The degree of managerial autonomy given to each family member in managing his or her department or function in the business.

There are some specific questions that would typically be on the minds of a family like the Leonards at this stage of their evolution. These would include family issues as well as business ones.

Where once every element of the business reported to Stew, Sr., as the entrepreneurial founder, now a different organization will be necessary. How will the reporting relationships operate between departments such as Bethy's Bakery, and stores such as the Danbury location, and functions such as Jill's Human Resources (team headquarters)?

Second, as new stores are begun and opened, business performance expectations, goals, and standards will need to be established. The standards for a new store rarely can be the same for an existing store. How do we establish the proper performance expectations for another family member in a new line of business?

If this question is not solved, there is a high risk of subjective evaluation of family managers based more on style than on results.

Third, will there be some limits to what is an incredibly powerful strategy? The greatest limit is the appetite of ownership to expand. The expansion strategy is so powerful, and there is so little to confine it. If you had to imagine some future issues regarding a business strategy, they might be some of the following:

Business Issues

- Will there be enough opportunities for fresh faces and ideas in the organization if the company's growth rate matures and the strong loyalty of people, the lower than usual turnover, and the promotion-from-within policies limit the opportunities to hire new people?
- Will the tenure and success of the employees eventually force the company to pay a noncompetitively high wage rate?
- Will the escalating costs and values of real estate and building construction reduce future financial returns?

Some future family issues that might be appropriate for expert consultation might be as follows:

Family Issues

- Who should lead and organize family meetings?
- Who would attend those meetings? All ten of the related family, or only those in the business, or only those related by blood, or only the four siblings?
- Should there be several types of family meetings—some for the Leonards, some for those in the business, some for just the siblings, and some for all?
- How much should the tremendous optimism and positivism of the family be challenged in family meetings to anticipate normal, predictable family conflicts or problems?
- How can the Leonards best integrate the in-laws into their powerful family and business culture when it is most likely that they come from a very different background?
- How soon and how much should the future vision of the business be structured?
- What size and number of store locations might the vision have?
- How geographically close will each business be?

- How should they organize the relationships between store managers, department managers, and functional managers?
- Should all the stores be interdependently related or more loosely related with separate equity structures?

In Summary

Stew Leonard's is a widely revered business. The Leonard family is an enchanting, exciting clan all working together in the family business. Perhaps their greatest strength is the tremendous thirst they have to learn as individuals and as a family. They read family business literature aggressively. They attend family business conferences and seminars. They are willing to hire family business experts for their opinions.

As eternal optimists and positivists, they will resist looking for problems, anticipate family conflict, and address and develop approaches to resolve problems among themselves. But surely their optimism, enthusiasm, and abundant playful fun time together will also be a source of great strength.

We are grateful to the Stew Leonard family for allowing us to observe them in their family business experience, and for the brilliant analysis by Professor John Ward.

Family Business Goes to the Movies

Let's take a look now at a somewhat less ideal situation, from the most popular movie on family business ever, *The Godfather*. By highlighting a few scenes from this romantic version of the life story of one of New York's five crime families, we can uncover the generally accepted folklore about what really goes on in a family business. After all, movies and plays must reflect some degree of truth for their works to receive wide acceptance.

The dramatic transition of power between the father, Don Corleone (Marlon Brando) and his son Michael (Al Pacino), who becomes the new godfather, captures in an exaggerated fashion some of the principles of family business we've discussed. Author Mario Puzo condenses the essence of family business into these four principles.

FIRST PRINCIPLE. The offspring least likely to be a successor usually ends up running the business. Therefore, you can never overtrain even the least likely.

In *The Godfather*, it was always assumed that the oldest son, Sonny Corleone (played by James Caan), would eventually control the business. As the oldest, he was trained and groomed for this control, he was expected to accept it, and he acted as if it were his birthright. The daughter, the middle child among three sons, was never expected to assume a key position in the business and the youngest son, Michael—who became the actual heir—was judged least likely to enter the family business. He was purposefully excluded from the inner secrets of the business from birth. The family felt Michael should be above the dirty nature of the family business. He was raised to be a doctor or lawyer or something equally special, certainly not "head crook." Isn't that level of family love for the youngest child heartwarming?

The third son, Freddie, was incompetent and never considered by the family for the stewardship of the business. He spent his time trying to make love to all the cocktail waitresses in Las Vegas. He was depicted as weak, and it was assumed to be the family's responsibility to give him a job under the family norm: "The weak we shall provide for."

Michael, who was as talented as Freddie was untalented, was kept out of the business and sent to college. He also became a war hero, demonstrating early success outside of the family business.

When the family business situation shifted suddenly and all hell broke loose (as does happen in the real world), and the competitors—the other mob—shot up Don Corleone, Michael suddenly had to become involved because the attack was not only on the business but on his father. Immediately, we see how family and business cannot be separated. In the ensuing strife, Sonny, the oldest son and heir-apparent, is murdered. Michael thus inherits control of the business. After all, the business had to be kept in the family.

This really is a classic case; it almost always seems that the least likely offspring eventually assumes the stewardship of a family business, so you can never overtrain the least likely. Otherwise, this offspring will have to assume an immense burden and intense risks, all at the wrong time and all without proper prior training.

A real-world example is the case of Seagram president Edgar Bronfman, Jr. As the second son, Edgar, Jr., never went to college; and until his father wooed him to Seagram, he knew next to nothing about the business. After only seven years, he rose through key business positions to become president, but, although he has already won respect among many competitors, some still snicker seeing Bronfman's latest promotion as one huge case of nepotism.

A tennis player is usually much better if he played tennis regularly as he was growing up. Someone who learns to play tennis in his mid-thirties just doesn't acquire the same skill as one who has played the game all his life. There are tremendous advantages to learning the basics during youth, just as it's easier for children to pick up foreign languages.

In a family business, it helps for the eventual champ to be acquainted with the business from day one. Statistics tell us only 80 percent of family businesses survive until the second generation, and a mere 20 percent survive until the third. Practice does not make perfect, rather, perfect practice makes perfect.

SECOND PRINCIPLE. To make the family business prosper, the successor may have to get rid of the in-laws.

Blood is thicker than water, and these days blood is certainly thicker than marriage. It is very difficult to be an in-law in a family-controlled business because, as we said in chapter 3, one's tenure is often contingent upon the success of the marriage. That's a shaky way to build a career.

In *The Godfather*, Mario Puzo sets up a classic trap: The murder of Sonny, it turns out, was contrived by the only son-in-law—the "no-good" who married the daughter. Michael, as the new head of the family business, has no choice but to kill his brother-in-law to maintain structure and discipline in the business.

This incident could have been portrayed as revenge, but the movie depicts the murder as a family cleansing where the only solution was to shoot the "out-laws." Puzo here feeds the viewer's natural uneasy feeling about in-laws. He leaves the viewer with no choice. It's just the way it is, you conclude. This situation is exaggerated, of course, but it is not unusual for some family business members to feel that the only choice is "All in-laws must go."

THIRD PRINCIPLE. It is sometimes better to lie in a family business than to tell the whole truth.

Probably the finest moment in *The Godfather* was the last scene. It depicts the best method of handling impossible conflict when there is no good choice. Just after Michael has his brother-in-law executed, Michael's sister enters the room and confronts him. She screams at him, accuses him of murdering her husband, and calls him a cold, heartless person with no feelings for her children, who are now fatherless. To think that Michael, who had just become godfather to these same children, would have their father killed, makes the act merciless. Talk about a tough management dilemma!

After the sister's tirade, Michael is left to face his own wife, who has witnessed the heated verbal exchange with her mouth hanging open. She shouts something like, "Michael, did you have our brother-in-law killed? You are a no-good heartless person." Puzo does his finest work here, showing how to handle the most difficult kinds of confrontations in family businesses—the ones that threaten to destroy both the family and the business in one swoop. Solve one of these wrong and there goes everything.

Michael immediately turns to his wife, slams his fist hard on the desk, looks into her eyes and says, "I thought we had an agreement in this family never to discuss business, never, ever, ever, under no circumstances. Do you remember that agreement?" See how graciously Puzo has Michael diffuse this confrontation?

His wife answers, "Yes, but this is no ordinary circumstance."

After a long pause, Michael responds, "Well, in that case, I'll violate this sacred rule this one time, and I will discuss business. But only this one time. Never again, OK?"

And his wife says, "OK, did you have our brother-in-law killed?"

Michael looks her straight in the eye and says, "No," firmly, emphatically, and convincingly.

The principle portrayed by Puzo here is that sometimes it is better to lie than to tell the whole truth when you own a family business. The idea is that the entrepreneur plays by the rules when he wins, and changes the rules when he loses—so he can win. It's not just doing things right in business, it's doing the right thing.

FOURTH PRINCIPLE. The founder of the business, the "old man," possesses business instincts that can never be gained from books or schooling. It's his job to pass this knowledge on to the kids.

In his role as the Godfather, Marlon Brando handles the difficult task of succession masterfully. The transition of Don Corleone from godfather to adviser and counselor to his son Michael, the new boss, echoes the role a board of directors or a trusted outside consultant would play in a family business. Michael has to reassign his former counselor, played by Robert Duvall, to make room for the Don.

The father constantly reminds Michael, for example, that the opposition would eventually seek to set up a "friendly" meeting. Even as his senility increases, the father continues to repeat, "If there is a member of the family who approaches you about that initial meeting, he will be the one that betrays you. Remember that." Over the course of the movie, Puzo works in that advice repeatedly.

Years later, an associate approaches Michael to set up a so-called "friendly" meeting and is indeed someone about to betray him. Michael has to arrange the killing of this former friend to protect the business.

The transfer of critical knowledge from the senior to the junior generation is a crucial element of family business survival. The principle here is that this critical knowledge can never be emphasized enough (and must not be diluted by barrels of trivial stuff) and that it's the job of the senior person to be 100-percent sure the junior person gets the message at all costs.*

We've taken four principles of family business and shown how brilliantly they were interwoven into this colorful movie. Rethink these principles as you reread our book and review *The Godfather*. They represent ideas that make up the prevailing wisdom about family businesses. Whether true or false, they have a strong impact, because they are interwoven into our society.

Bonus Principle. Every family business should have a "godfather." This principle is not drawn from the movie, but is still a sound practice. This "godfather" is a person who is trusted and respected by all the family and could serve as a mediator should that become necessary. He or she should be unbiased and have little or no vested interest in the company. The godfather can be a business acquaintance, friend, college professor, or someone respected in the field. Bring this person into the picture right at the beginning and keep him informed. This is not the sort of person you can find in the middle of a crisis.

If you are unusually lucky, you may never need "the godfather" to do more than settle minor disputes or serve as a sounding board for new ideas. If the worst comes to pass, though, and the business must be dissolved, this person may be the only one who can keep the pieces together long enough for the business to regain its equilibrium and survive. Nothing lasts forever, but the business, if it survives at all, will probably outlive the closeness and trust the original family counted on as it was building the business.

* At a recent CEO Club event in Manhattan, one of the lifetime members was asked a question during a ten-minute new-member introduction. He responded matter-of-factly with no pause. His answer is worth repeating. His name is Rick Globus, and along with his twin brother, Steve, they manage a well-known venture capital pool called The Globus Growth Group. Rick described himself as the long-haired, flaky brother, as compared to his straighter, more numbers-oriented, shorter-haired twin. The question was, "How did you learn the venture capital business—did you go to business school?" Rick said, "Not really, I learned all I know from my dad, who started the business. Just hanging around the house taught me more than I learned any other way, including business school."

The Guccis: Who's on First?

A real-life Italian family business is that of the Gucci family, whose members have probably spent more time rushing *into* court than the Corleones did trying to stay out. Creators of the finest in fashions, the Gucci family has been anything but harmonious. Three generations of bitter feuding pitted father against son, uncle against nephew, cousin against cousin. After more than twenty lawsuits, the empire has passed to Maurizio Gucci, grandnephew of the founder, but he has ahead of him the daunting task of restoring the luster to the oversold Gucci name.

The company, founded in 1923 by Guccio Gucci, a leather goods craftsman whose initials form the firm's internationally recognized logo of interlocking Gs, emphasized Florentine quality and tight family control. After Mussolini invaded Ethiopia in 1935, the League of Nations sanctions cut Guccio off from his main source of leather. He designed a line of canvas luggage adorned with his initials and the family mark was born. The two Gs have been a golden goose ever since.

Of Guccio's three sons, only Aldo, the oldest, really jumped into the business. After his first visit to the United States, Aldo pursued overseas expansion, opening 180 stores abroad, which account for 82 percent of the parent company's sales. Aldo, in turn, brought his three sons, Giorgio, Paolo, and Roberto, and his nephew Maurizio (who inherited his father Rodolfo's 50 percent of the shares) into the business.

In 1982, the family was irrevocably split. When Paolo proposed the marketing of inexpensive items under the Gucci name, he was ousted from the company during an explosive board meeting. Paolo sued the family for $13.3 million in the New York courts, claiming that Aldo, assisted by Roberto, Giorgio, and Maurizio, had struck him with the tape recorder he had sneaked into the meeting. He more effectively alleged that his father, Aldo, had evaded U.S. taxes. Aldo was forced to admit his evasion and received a one-year jail sentence from the U.S. government. Meanwhile, nephew Maurizio used his 50-percent share to seize control of the company and oust Uncle Aldo. He brought in a new team of managers to help run the company professionally.

Maurizio's initial reign was short-lived. Aldo's other sons, Giorgio and Roberto, countersued, claiming Maurizio's shares were based on forged documents and also charging *him* with tax evasion. The Italian government, having had just about enough, stepped in, freezing Maurizio's shares and appointing Maria Martellini, a professor of economics from Milan's Bocconi school, to replace him as a state custodian. She told the family point-blank, according to a piece by Nancy Marx Better in *Manhattan, Inc.* magazine, ". . . for the sake of the Gucci operation, they should keep their own problems away from the company. Gucci is not a family business anymore. It is not vital to have a family member working for the company." Under state-controlled management, the company expanded production, standardizing the quality of its stores and trimming its product line.

While in exile, Maurizio plotted. In late 1987, Morgan Stanley hooked him up with Investcorp, a Bahrain-based group that specializes in acquiring troubled companies and turning them around. Investcorp makes messy situations like the Guccis' their business. Using Morgan Stanley as a conduit, Investcorp acquired the other Guccis' holdings, and brought back Maurizio as chairman of the company.

One of Maurizio's first moves was to put his father Rodolfo's right-hand man, Domenico De Sole, in charge of the American operation. De Sole is a classic example of the "trusted lieutenant" we discuss in chapter 5. It is even rumored that on his deathbed Rodolfo made De Sole promise to take care of Maurizio, who is five years his junior. Another "outside adviser" brought in by Maurizio was Dawn Mello, former president of Bergdorf Goodman. Her responsibility was to create a new in-house design team to restore the luster to the faded Gucci name.

After years of feuding, Maurizio is finally heading the company, having vanquished the rest of the family, but his position is not yet secure. For one, he'll have to make sure his outside advisers, De Sole and Mello, don't start feuding themselves. Some people suggest, after all, that Maurizio brought in Mello to show De Sole who was boss. De Sole was not even invited to interview her. And then there's Investcorp hovering in the background, capable of selling the firm again to another private buyer, or forcing a public sale.

As we pointed out in chapter 7, it is important that partners establish firm guidelines for the purchase of the stock of a partner who dies, because the heirs do not generally share the level of camaraderie and loyalty the founders of the company enjoyed and nurtured as they developed the business.

The Binghams of Louisville, Kentucky

As we mentioned earlier in this chapter, some family business decisions hurt the family and some the business, but occasionally a situation develops that threatens to destroy both. The Gucci internecine struggle clearly destroyed the family, but the business has managed to survive. The Binghams of Louisville were not so lucky.

As many readers probably already know from the press reports of her story and the three books recounting it, Sarah "Sallie" Bingham used her stock to force the sale of the Bingham newspaper empire because she felt her ideas and her 15 percent of the companies were not being considered. Her parents had given her the stock, feeling strongly that the company must be divided equally among the children. Had they given her something else of equal value, the company might have stayed in the family. We discussed in chapter 2 the dangers to a family business of putting ideals of familial loyalty above what's best for the business.

The Binghams repeatedly made that mistake, and it led over time directly to the downfall of the business and the dissolution of family ties.

According to David Leon Chandler's provocative book, *The Binghams of Louisville: The Dark History Behind One of America's Great Fortunes*, Barry Bingham began working on the papers as a police reporter in 1930 and became acting publisher when his father and owner of the papers, Robert Worth Bingham, was appointed ambassador to Great Britain. Upon Robert's death in 1937, Barry became publisher of the *Courier-Journal* and the *Louisville Times*. He also upgraded the Bingham radio station, eventually opened one of the first television stations, WHAS, and ran the profitable Standard Gravure printing company. By all accounts he was a fine (though autocratic) publisher; and under his direction the newspapers became a journalistic institution of the nation, taking the lead on a variety of liberal causes such as civil rights, opposition to the Vietnam War, and environmental concerns.

Barry and his wife, Richmond belle Mary Caperton, had five children: Worth, Barry, Jr., Sallie, Jonathan, and Eleanor. The firstborn, Worth, was carefully groomed for succession, violating the "don't put all your eggs in one basket" principle we discussed early in this chapter with regard to the Corleones. Sure enough, Worth was killed in a freak accident when he was thirty-four, leaving his unprepared younger brother Barry, Jr., to run the company (youngest son Jonathan died at twenty-one of accidental electrocution). Barry, Jr., gave up the television career he had been planning and agreed to prepare himself to take over as editor and publisher of the newspapers. He succeeded his father as CEO after Barry, Sr., retired in 1971, retaining a position as chairman of the boards of the family companies.

During the sixties and seventies, the Bingham daughters, Eleanor and Sallie, left Louisville to pursue their own interests, as neither had ever been considered even as potential paper boys! Each daughter made a mark for herself, Eleanor producing television documentaries and Sallie winning awards for her fiction and book contracts. With such aptitude, Sallie might have made valuable contributions to the family business instead of becoming the agent of its destruction.

In the late seventies, both daughters returned to Louisville, Eleanor to raise her children and Sallie to nurse the wounds of her two failed marriages. Their return prompted Barry, Sr., to make a fatal mistake. Fearing what he termed "the grandchildren syndrome," whereby the sheer number of third-generation owners splits the business apart, he made the two daughters voting members of the boards of the family companies. Going whole-hog against another vital principle of our book (chapter 5: appoint an objective board of *outside* directors), he also appointed his wife, Worth's widow, and Junior's wife to the board.

If you've read chapter 5 carefully, you'll predict instant conflict between a board composed of Mom, the Old Man, and family members with no experience running the family business or any business, and the CEO, Barry, Jr. You would be correct. Conflict broke out almost immediately, with Barry, Jr., accusing the board of Monday-morning quarterbacking and board members, particularly the sisters, demanding more information and more control.

After Sallie began making public comments alleging sexism at the Bingham companies, her parents tried to mollify her by adding her to the newspaper staff as a book editor, at an entry-level salary. She and her sister continued to have sharp disagreements at board meetings with Barry about the papers' political endorsements, editorials, and operation.

In 1980, Barry, Jr., insisted that all board members sign a buy-back agreement stipulating that should they receive an outside offer to sell their stock, the Bingham companies would have sixty days to match the offer. Sallie was the only member to refuse to sign. Three years later Barry, Jr., issued an ultimatum: Either the women left the board or he would resign. He had reached this point, he said, after consulting with Leon Danco, who told him he needed a professional board of directors, not family members with no business experience (sound familiar?). Sallie refused to budge.

Barry, Jr., offered a compromise: He would turn over management of the companies to a group of nonfamily professional managers. Barry, Sr., refused to allow it, saying that the companies might as well be sold if Binghams were not going to manage them. Finally, Sallie was voted off the boards in March of 1984, while all the other women resigned and Sallie shocked the family by announcing that she would sell her stock to outside bidders.

In July, in an effort to end the family feud, Sallie offered to sell her 15-percent share to the family. This plan was soon derailed, however, when the family's investment bank appraised her shares at around $25 million, while her own private appraisers estimated their value at over $80 million. Accordingly, she resumed her plan to sell to outsiders.

In a countermove, Barry, Jr., offered to allow Eleanor, who was by this time also disgruntled, to run WHAS, the TV station, on the condition that she convince Sallie to sell at the family price. Eleanor eventually agreed, but only if the family could reach an agreement with Sallie on a price. She dropped her price to $32 million; Barry, Jr., countered with a refusal to go above $26.3 million. At this point Barry, Sr., stepped in to announce he had had just about enough and was selling all the companies to regain peace in the family and ensure financial security for future generations. Sallie's share of the total sale came to about $82 million, with her stock worth more than twice what she had been offered by Barry, Jr.

The Bingham experience is unfortunately familiar. When gifts of stock are made to children, future battle lines are drawn between inactive shareholders and active family managers of the business. The natural tendency is for the passive shareholders to be intolerant of the business decisions made by the "insiders" and for the insiders to see the "outsiders" as parasites who don't know what they're talking about.

Many parents unwisely give equal shares of voting common stock to active and inactive children. Annual gifts of voting stock make tax sense but don't create a good long-term environment for the business. On the other hand, nonvoting preferred and common shares for inactive children are not the answer, either, as children deprived of a voice in company affairs are at the mercy of those running the business. Instead, give the child who won't be working in the business other assets.

Any family business owner determined to give voting stock to passive and active children must seriously consider establishing an outside board of directors. Without a board of directors that genuinely represents all shareholders—active and inactive—most families will not be able to resolve the mistrust and power issues such stock arrangements engender.

One final note: Whatever position you hold in your family's business, be wary of asking your lawyer to speak for you to other family members. Try to keep your family members communicating directly with each other. Once the lawyers start picking up the phones, the risk of family war escalates. Keep your lawyer abreast of developments and heed her advice, but keep her out of family discussions unless actual buying and selling is being considered.

Johnson Versus Johnson

When dyslexic billionaire J. Seward Johnson signed virtually his entire $500-million estate over to his third wife in his last will, he set off a vicious court battle among his heirs. In her book *Johnson v. Johnson*, Barbara Goldsmith speculates that the heirs to the Johnson pharmaceutical fortune were fighting less over money than over the love they never had from their manipulative father. Goldsmith writes: "J. Seward Johnson's behavior toward his children—his patterns of rejection and divisiveness—ultimately led them into a courtroom seeking to find what they had never had from him: recognition, a sense of worthiness, and a measure of a father's love. Perhaps restitution for this loss came to be equated with money."

In his final will, signed on April 14, 1983—thirty-nine days before his death—Johnson disinherited his children and even cut out a bequest to his favorite charity. The woman to whom he left his estate, Basia Piasecka Johnson, married him when she was thirty-four and he was seventy-six. She was employed as a cook/chambermaid by his second wife, and they were married eight days after Johnson's divorce from his second wife was final.

The six Johnson children, Elaine, James, Mary Lea, J. Seward Jr., Diana, and Jennifer, promptly contested the will—their lawyers charging Basia with shattering Johnson's second marriage and dominating him.

Basia's lawyers countered that Johnson had left her the bulk of his estate because he loved her, wanted to avoid paying unnecessary taxes, and was fed up with the profligate and wasted lives of his children. The lawyers also noted that Johnson had established trusts in 1944 for his children worth roughly $600 million and claimed Johnson felt his children had enough money and had not done much with what they'd already been given. Both sets of lawyers vied with each other to expose the seamiest of the family scandals.

According to Goldsmith, the trial was the longest, the most sensational, and the most expensive will contest in U.S. history. Two hundred and ten lawyers had a hand in the litigation, which ended in this settlement:

- To each child: $6.2 million after taxes, and an extra $8 million to Seward Jr. for his lost executor and trusteeship fees.
- To Harbor Branch, Seward's favorite charity during his life: $20 million.
- To Basia: all charges of fraud, etc., dropped, and a $350-million bonus.
- Basia's lawyer, Nina Zagat: all charges of fraud, etc., dropped plus $1.8 million before taxes.
- Lawyers' fees: around $24 million.
- The IRS: around $86 million in taxes.

The *Johnson v. Johnson* case is clearly the story of a family business run amok.

Although J. Seward Johnson was a passive, second-generation inheritor who left the running of Johnson & Johnson to his older brother, Robert "the General" Johnson, his life and the lives of his heirs were profoundly affected (even ruined) by the family business.

To accumulate his massive fortune, Seward sat back and watched his stock appreciate. By all accounts, he was an isolated, introverted, sickly child, partly because his dyslexia—a little-understood condition in those days—was so severe as to render him functionally illiterate. Remember when we pointed out that a strong parent has either very strong or very weak offspring. In the Johnson case, founder Robert Johnson had both, and Seward was the very weak one.

Seward was abandoned by his mother, who took off for England after a female friend of hers kidnapped him and held him for ten days in her Park Avenue apartment for sexual purposes until his older brother (the strong offspring) rescued him. Throughout his life Seward displayed out-of-control sexuality: Not only was he consistently unfaithful to various wives, he molested his daughter Mary Lea from age nine to sixteen.

Johnson & Johnson is composed of 160 companies, marketing health-care products in 150 countries, with $6.4 billion annually in sales as of Goldsmith's writing in 1987. The company became a source of tremendous unearned wealth for the children and grandchildren of the founders, Edward Mead and James Wood Johnson. Two years after its inception in 1883, older brother Robert invested his interest in another company in Johnson & Johnson. He soon replaced James as president and the company concentrated on utilizing Joseph Lister's methods of sterilization (Lister had identified airborne germs as a source of infection) to produce antiseptic surgical dressings.

When Robert died, his son Robert took over the business and became surrogate father to his younger brother Seward after their mother abandoned them. Certain themes run repeatedly through the story of this family business: domination by an older brother, sexism and secretiveness, and an "image of purity and Christian piety concealing self-indulgent behavior," according to Goldsmith.

Seward was openly content to allow his brother to run the family business. He told his daughter Mary Lea, "You can't have two captains of a ship. My brother's the captain of Johnson & Johnson." He did parlay his love of boats and sailing into forays around the globe that convinced him to encourage the global expansion of the company that Robert undertook.

It was Seward's passivity, though, that allowed Robert to take the company all the way. He had Seward's complete loyalty and confidence and apparently recognized how valuable this cooperation was: "I think the most important decision was one my brother and I made jointly to develop confidence in each other. We felt the possibilities of this company were unlimited so long as we maintained this confidence in each other." The Binghams should have been so lucky.

For whatever psychological reasons, Seward never built this sort of relationship with his own children. Through mental and sexual abuse, he broke them down and discouraged them from entering the family business. The children of his first wife, Seward, Mary Lea, Diana, and Elaine, lived at one point in a rat-infested garage attached to a chicken coop on the grounds of Merriewold, the family mansion.

From the children's testimony during the contesting of their father's will, it is clear that his final complete rejection of them shattered dreams they still held on to of being loved and accepted by him. Indeed, their attempt to make a scapegoat of Basia is further testimony to the resiliency of the hope abused children seem able to hold on to in the face of overwhelming evidence that they are not loved.

As Goldsmith wrote: "The legacy that Seward Johnson was to leave his children was one of abundant inherited wealth and nothing more—no work ethic, no stress on education, little religion."

In fairness to Seward, we should note that his own childhood, fraught with neglect and abandonment, hardly prepared him to be anything but a rotten father. The Johnson family consistently used its vast wealth to cover up its problems, from Seward's dyslexia to his sexual profligacy, his children's suicide attempts, and marital problems. As long as the business ticked along under Robert's command and the dividends rolled in, family members could run wild.

The lesson of *Johnson v. Johnson* should be taken to heart by any parent/owner of a family business or, for that matter, by any parent. It's a lesson on the nature of vacuums. If money is all you offer your children when their needs for values, education, and moral support are not filled, they may think they're living a swell life, but they won't be.

In his bestseller, *Inside the Family Business*, Leon Danco notes: "The successful founder and his family must be able to accept a rapid rise in socio-economic status without being destroyed in the process . . . and, he must be able to pass this ability on to his family so that they can expand socially without destroying existing friendships or values."

W. K. Vanderbilt put it more succinctly: "Inherited wealth is a big handicap to happiness. It is as certain death to ambition as cocaine is to morality."

Parents should consider planning how their children and grandchildren will receive the wealth from the family business very carefully. The first step is to recognize what a "big handicap" inherited wealth can be. The second step for a parent/owner might be to decide what he or she would want to see children do with the money and plan the distribution of wealth accordingly. Some states have set up special educational investment schemes, for example. According to a recent piece in *U.S. News & World Report* (May 7, 1990), Michigan, Wyoming, Wisconsin, and Florida have sold more than $775 million in prepaid tuition packages for in-state public colleges and universities since 1988.

Trusts are another option that is no longer just for the ultrarich. A living trust can be created, leaving detailed instructions about distribution of assets. A credit-shelter trust, which allows each parent to pass on $600,000 separately tax-free to their children, is another option. Such trusts can be set up so a surviving spouse may receive income and principal from it, as well. Trusts for children can also be set up with conditions for distribution of money, such as requiring a child to be gainfully employed or have completed college, according to *U.S. News*.

Money alone can keep someone happy for only so long. Maybe that's why family businesses—which offer the chance to combine familial love and values with the harsher realities of business—are worth all the trouble and effort.

It's strange but true that those people constituted to make a lot of money are also psychologically constituted not to enjoy it, and those able to enjoy it are usually not capable of making it. As J. D. Rockfeller, Jr. said, "I was born into it and there was nothing I could do about it. It was there, like air or food or any other element. *The only question with wealth is what to do with it.*"

There's a Ford in Their Future

The first Ford (William) arrived in the United States from Ireland in 1832 and settled in what is now Dearborn, Michigan. He selected Dearbornville simply because it happened to be the first clearing along the forest route Indian tribes had been traversing between the Detroit River and Chicago.

William Ford's dream was to farm his own land, a privilege denied him in the old country. He married Mary Litogot in 1861 and built their farm home in the midst of a forest.

Henry I

Henry Ford I was born in 1863. Actually, Henry was the second child born to the couple, as their first died at birth in 1862. This little baby, in my opinion, became the world's greatest entrepreneur of his time.

Henry attended the single-room Dearborn school, where he was an average student; however, his genius-level mechanical ability manifested itself at an early age. At seven, young Henry saw the insides of a watch for the first time and became obsessed with repairing watches. After visiting a file company in Detroit, he returned home to make his own file, and used it to shape his mother's corset stays into miniature screwdrivers. He was always a clever and enterprising child. "To judge from his own recollections in his notebooks, and in the numerous second-hand accounts, the young Henry Ford was forever dismantling, investigating, and generally displaying his mechanical genius in all directions."*

As happens even today, Henry's father was appalled when his son rejected the

* from *Ford: The Men & the Machine*, by Robert Lacey (Little, Brown, 1986), p. 10.

possibility of working the family soil. "To the elder Ford, on his own land at last, free of the old country, the farm was liberating; to Henry Ford, bored and restless, it was like a prison."*

One of the most traumatic events in the young Ford's life was the death of his mother when he was twelve. The depth of this mourning manifested itself in many ways late in Henry's adult life. He cherished the lessons he ascribed to her.

"Mother taught me disagreeable jobs call for courage and patience and self-discipline, and she taught me also that 'I don't want to' gets a fellow nowhere. . . .

"My mother used to say when I grumbled about it, 'Life will give you many unpleasant tasks . . . Your duty will be hard and disagreeable and painful to you at times, but you must do it. You may have pity on others, but you must not pity yourself.' "** Ford made many references to his mother's influence on him during the rest of his life, including the quote, "I have tried to live my life as my mother would have wished."

"A few months after his mother's death (July 1876) the young Henry was riding with his father in a horse-drawn wagon when he saw a steam engine coming towards him propelled by its own power. This was the first vehicle not drawn by horses that Henry Ford had ever seen. (In retrospect, what a momentuous occasion this was for the entire world.)

"These engines were common sights on American farms by the end of the nineteenth century. They were used to carry power via broad webbing belts running around the drive wheel to threshing machines, corn huskers, or circular saws. This one, however, was unique because a chain made a connection between the engine and rear wheels of the wagonlike frame on which the boiler was mounted. The chain enabled the steam engine to move itself under its own power."***

This was Henry Ford's first encounter with the horseless carriage, which was to bring him and his heirs fame and fortune far beyond the dreams of a young farm boy in Dearborn, Michigan.

In December of 1879, Henry Ford (age seventeen) left for Detroit, where he worked for a high-quality machine shop. As an apprentice, he became immersed in machinery, working among men who, like himself, thought only of the future applications of machines. He earned $2.50 a week, which left him $1 short of meeting his weekly living expenses. To make up the deficit, he took to repairing watches in the evening for a jewelry store.

* from *The Reckoning*, by David Halberstam (Morrow, 1986, $19.95), p. 73.

** Lacey, p. 11.

*** Ibid., p. 12.

To jump ahead a hundred years, Henry Ford's grandson Henry II, who everyone says was a chip off the old block, ran the Ford empire for several decades. Henry II's second wife, in a highly publicized divorce, was awarded among other things $5,000 a week for life for cut flowers in her home! While you may think that extravagant, it's only a quarter of a million annually. When compared to the original founder (Henry I), the difference between $1 and the wealth created is like night and day. "Henry Ford's fascination with watches led him to what he was sure was a brilliant idea. He would invent a watch so simple it could be mass-produced. Two thousand a day would come off a simple assembly line at a cost of only 30 cents each. He was absolutely certain he could design and produce the watch; the only problem, he decided, was in marketing 600,000 watches a year. It was not a challenge that appealed to him, so he dropped the project, but the basic idea of simplifying a product in order to mass-produce it stayed with him."*

After five years in Detroit, Henry was enticed back to the farm with an offer of forty acres of timberland, a gift from his father to rescue his wayward son from the city and his damnable machines. Henry Ford took it because he momentarily needed security—he was about to marry Clara Bryant. As history shows, fathers like to bring their wayward children into the family business, and many of them resort to bribery to make it happen.

However, nothing convinced Henry more of his love of machines than the drudgery of being back on the farm. He continued to spend every spare minute tinkering and inventing. He experimented with the sawmill; he tried to invent a steam engine for a plow. Crude stationary gasoline engines had been developed, and he was sure a new world of gasoline-powered machines was about to arrive. He desperately wanted to be part of it. Positive that important new inventions were just around the corner, he told his wife Clara they were going back to Detroit. And Henry was the head of the house.

His father continued to worry about him, saying, "He just doesn't seem to settle down, I don't know what will become of him." How many fathers have said these exact words?

Upon Henry and Clara's return to Detroit, he found talented machinists chasing the same dream of building a gasoline-powered automobile. Henry sold his first car for $200 and used the money to immediately start the next. "Henry Ford had been encouraged by his hero, Thomas Edison, whom he had met at a convention. Edison had asked the young Ford a series of pointed questions. Then, after Ford had sketched out his ideas, Edison told him, 'Young man, that's the thing! You have it—the self-contained unit carrying its own fuel with it! Keep at it!' That was all the encouragement he needed, particularly since it came

* Halberstam, p. 74.

from the great Edison, and it provided the life-long fuel to carry through several bankruptcies."*

Henry's first partner was Alexander Malcolmson, the first of several early fortunate investors. (Malcolmson's bookkeeper James Couzens sold out his $2,500 initial investment to Ford in 1919 for $29 million.) However, Ford and Malcolmson split over the direction of the company. Malcolmson was for building fancy cars, the most popular of the times, while Henry wanted to build plain sturdy cars for the multitudes.

Ford's theory on building automobiles was "to make one automobile just like another automobile; just as one pin is like another pin, or one match is like another match when they come from a factory. Henry wanted to make many cars at a low price. 'Better and cheaper,' he would say. 'More of them, better and cheaper.' "**

It was the coming of the Model T in 1908 that sent Ford's career skyrocketing. With the Model T, the modern industrial age—the Industrial Age that benefited rather than exploited the common person—began.

Model Ts were built on an innovative creation of Henry Ford's that became the universal method for building automobiles: the assembly line. And as the mass production increased, Henry Ford *decreased* the price of his car from the initial $780 in 1910 to $360 in 1917. By 1920, the company was earning $6 million a month after taxes and sold as many cars as the rest of the manufacturers combined. To accomplish such an overwhelming feat is beyond logic. It takes an unusual survivor with deep commitments and a clever mind to achieve this accomplishment in human history. To also think that this person can simultaneously be a great father or husband is like asking a great prizefighter to also be a great pianist. In some ways the skills needed to be a great entrepreneur are opposite those needed to be a compassionate, reasoning person, and Henry Ford was the world's greatest entrepreneur!

Another example of Ford's creative genius was the Rouge plant, "a totally independent industrial city-state" capable of supplying steel, glass, and engines to the assembly lines. Iron-ore barges would unload their cargo into the industrial complex, and thirty-three hours later it would all come out as engines. In later years, Eiji Toyoda of the Toyota company said, "There is no secret how we learned our just-in-time Japanese manufacturing theory, which is so admired by American automobile manufacturers. We learned it at the Ford Rouge."

The dehumanization of the automobile manufacturing workplace because of the relentless speed of the assembly line created serious morale problems among

* Halberstam, p. 76.

** Ibid., p. 78.

the workers. The labor turnover rate at one point was 380 percent. In order to keep 400 men working, Ford had to hire more than 1,000. In keeping with Henry Ford's simplistic methods of problem-solving, he shocked the entire industrial world by establishing his famous $5 per day pay plan for Ford assembly line workers, which *doubled* their existing rate of pay. It is an example of how entrepreneurs can go against the grain.

Ford wasn't so kind in all aspects of employee treatment, however. Firings were often cruel and brutal. Foremen on the assembly line were increasingly chosen for their physical strength rather than mechanical ability. If a worker appeared to be loitering, the foreman simply knocked him down.

Ford's chief of security, the infamous Harry Bennett, whose inhuman acts of cruelty for the Ford Motor Company are legendary, was Henry's "muscle." The darkest deeds attributed to Henry Ford were usually carried out by Bennett.

One incident involved one of Ford's top engineers, who had lost favor with Henry and had been turned over to Bennett for dismissal. The man, Frank Kulick, was asked to listen to an alleged faulty magneto in a car idling in the factory. Kulick climbed up on the fender to listen, and as he did, Bennett drove the car out into the yard beyond the gate. Turning the car sharply, Kulick was thrown to the ground, whereupon Bennett raced back into the factory and locked the gates. Kulick was never allowed inside again.

Henry Ford hated bookkeepers and accountants. He didn't like lawyers, either, but he just plain hated the accountants. In fact, while passing through an office filled with white-collar workers, he instructed an aide to fire the entire group, claiming, "They're not productive, they don't do any real work, they're parasites!"

Ford once told a noted historian, "A great business is really too big to be human."

There was no question about Henry Ford's despotic management style. He once returned from a lengthy trip to Europe and found his engineers had tampered with his Model T by making a few small improvements. They had improved the riding qualities by lowering the car slightly, and lengthening it by twelve inches. They proudly showed Henry the new improved car upon his return. "He walked around it several times. Finally he approached the left-hand door and ripped it off. Then he ripped off the other door. Then he smashed the windshield. Then he threw out the back seat and bashed in the roof with his shoe. During all this he said nothing. There was no doubt whose car the T was and no doubt who was the only man permitted to change it. For the next thirty years, anyone wanting to improve a Ford car ran into a stone wall."*

* Halberstam, p. 90.

Even an apparent minor (in those days) detail demonstrated the power of King Henry in the Ford Motor Company: "Any color, so long as it's black." Into this environment came the heir-designate Edsel Ford.

Edsel Ford

Edsel Ford was born in 1893, the only child of Henry and Clara Jane Bryant. He was a courteous and dutiful child, and displayed many of the engineering skills of his father.

After working for the company for six years, Edsel became president of the Ford Motor Company on December 31, 1918. He was twenty-six years old. His first responsibility as president was an important one. He was entrusted by his father to buy out all the other stockholders in the company, thereby making the company a true family business. After this reorganization in 1919, Edsel owned 40 percent of the shares.

As president, Edsel's office was located next to his father's in Highland Park. Edsel was a considerate and knowledgeable CEO. Unlike his father, he was patient with people and never abrupt. According to his secretary, A. J. Lepine, "He was an even-tempered man. One would practically never hear him say anything sarcastic or resentful about other people. . . . He had a way of expressing disapproval, if he did disapprove, by an attitude of silence. He kept himself uniformly under control."* Everyone was agreed, in a business not generally noted for breeding or refinement: Edsel Ford was a gentleman.

In 1916, Edsel married a Detroit socialite, Eleanor Clay. It soon became apparent that Eleanor Clay Ford brought a new and powerful personality into the Ford family. She immediately began to move her husband "out of the close smothering orbit of his parents, providing him with a context of his own, and it was Eleanor who helped Edsel to stand as a Ford in his own right."**

She was a blunt person who let one know what was on her mind. Edsel, on the other hand, was discreet, inhibited by a desire to be loving and caring, which severely debilitated him in dealing with his autocratic father. They had four children, Henry II (1917), Benson (1919), Josephine Clay (1923), and William Clay (1925).

Henry and only child Edsel had a close relationship while Edsel was growing up, and they both shared a love of machines and the successes that accrued to the family and the Ford Motor Company. Henry was very generous with money to Edsel, paying him an average of $3 million a year during the twenties. However,

* Lacey, p. 256.

** Ibid.

as Henry had demonstrated so often during his career, unexpectedly pulling the rug out from under business associates was a common occurrence, and his beloved son was not immune to this inhuman exercise.

Henry believed Edsel was weak and not able to handle the pressure of dealing with the threats from business associates and competitors. In his mind, he thought he needed to prepare his son for this eventuality by toughening him up. The problem was that the methods he used eventually broke Edsel's spirit. To many observers, Edsel's early death at forty-nine could be attributed to a broken heart at the hands of a loving but terribly misguided father.

There was a constant tug-of-war between Edsel and Henry over modernizing the Ford products as well as their factory facilities. Henry resisted installing hydraulic brakes for several years which, coupled with other modernized engineering features, gave their chief competitor, Chevrolet, a golden opportunity in the low-priced volume marketplace.

Once, Edsel had decided to expand the sales and accounting offices while Henry was away on a trip. When Henry returned, he questioned Edsel as to what was being built. Unwittingly, Edsel did not emphasize the need of the sales department for more space, but instead began by mentioning that the accounting department was a beneficiary of the expansion. Henry, as mentioned previously, hated bookkeepers. He didn't give Edsel a chance to finish and stormed out of the room. Henry never learned that the sales department was also being expanded.

The next morning when the accounting staff came to work, their existing offices had been stripped of all the furniture and equipment during the night. Later that day, it was learned that the entire department had been abolished by the elder Ford.

"It was the measure of Edsel Ford that, over the weeks following, he found jobs for every one of the sacked accountants, fitting them unobtrusively into other departments—and it was the measure of Henry Ford that he knew Edsel was doing this. There was a twisted collusion in the sad game that father and son were to play out through the twenties and thirties, and its cruelest twist was that time did not heal the process, it made it worse. The more Edsel submitted, the more his father hurt him, and the more the boy was wounded, the more submissive he became.

"Another incident concerned Edsel's involvement with Laurence Sheldrick, the company's chief engineer, in developing a six-cylinder engine. Edsel believed he had paternal permission to begin experimenting, even though Henry had opposed it for years, declaring, 'I've no use for an engine that has more spark plugs than a cow has teats.'

"Sheldrick and Edsel labored for six months and were delighted with the prototype. When they were about ready to test it, Sheldrick received a call from

Henry Ford. 'Sheldrick,' he said, 'I've got a new scrap conveyor that I'm very proud of. It goes right to the cupola at the top of the plant. I'd like you to come and take a look at it. I'm really proud of it.' "*

Sheldrick joined Ford at the top of the cupola, where they could watch the conveyor work. To Sheldrick's surprise, Edsel was there too. Soon the conveyor started. The first thing riding up on it, on its way to becoming junk, was Edsel Ford and Larry Sheldrick's engine.

"Now," said the old man, "don't you try anything like that again. Don't you ever, do you hear?"

In the final months of Edsel's life, malevolent Henry used the bestial Harry Bennett to complete the annihilation of his son. During this period, Bennett, who was Henry's closest associate in the company, harassed Edsel mercilessly, "to the old man's obvious pleasure."

After Edsel's death in 1943, the Ford Motor Company was in dire straits. Had it not been the middle of World War II, with its U.S. government contracts, the company might very well have gone under. The government needed the production capability of Ford to build war materials, and it was the intervention of the nation's highest officials who innocently preserved the company for Henry II, who was serving in the Navy.

Eleanor Clay Ford

Eleanor had been a witness to the destructive power of the elder Ford, and the Rasputin-like Bennett in making her a premature widow. She now sensed her senile father-in-law was in danger of turning the company over to Bennett, thereby cheating her son Henry II out of his birthright.

Bennett's debilitating reputation was well known to the government officials whose war effort depended on Ford's survival, so when Eleanor and Clara (Henry's wife) joined forces, requesting that Henry II be granted orders back to Detroit to run Ford with his grandfather, they agreed.

Henry II returned reluctantly, for his Navy career had granted him a taste of personal freedom from the family. He was named vice-president in December 1943, granting him titular power—and the power of blood, but unless his grandfather moved aside and Bennett left the company, he would never be able to take control. Again, Eleanor put her foot down and forced the issue. She threatened to sell her stock, 40 percent of the company inherited from Edsel, unless old Henry stepped aside in favor of his grandson. Henry's wife Clara supported her completely. They fought off the old man's excuses and delaying

* Halberstam, p. 100.

ploys. With the threat, and a sense these women were intensely serious, Henry Ford finally, furiously, gave up, and Henry II took control. Eleanor Clay Ford reigned as the "Queen Mother" of the Ford Royal Family for thirty-three years following the death of her husband, until her death in 1976.

Henry II—Successor-Designate

Though there were four children born to Edsel and Eleanor Clay Ford, Henry II, Benson, Josephine Clay, and William Clay, there was little doubt Henry II was the logical choice to lead the company. He was the oldest, and none of his siblings possessed his leadership qualities to challenge this transition. Benson inherited his father Edsel's sweet disposition, and he was content to let Henry run the company. Josephine, like other Ford women, never figured in the successorship process, and William was too young, so the mantle of power fell on Henry II's shoulders. Ultimately, Benson and his younger brother William assumed important positions in the management of the company "similar to what Eleanor (their mother) envisioned when she said they should sit at Henry II's right and left hands."*

Henry Ford II was an anomaly. He could spend hours carousing on the town with his friends, and the next morning he would be on the job bright-eyed and bushy-tailed. Woe to the drinking buddy who made the mistake of assuming the shared intimacy of the previous night of revelry gained special privileges in Ford's office. He inherited his grandfather's unpredictability in handling close associates. When Henry II got turned off on someone, the suddenness of his actions in ending business relationships would leave the victim stunned and broken.

The Lee Iaccocca incident is a perfect example of Henry's sharklike process, except that Iaccocca may have been stunned, but as history has proven, he was far from broken. The reasons for the dismissal of Lee Iaccocca as president of Ford were strictly personal irritations that Henry II experienced, and had little to do with his performance as president. In fact, Henry II had to threaten the board of directors, "It's either him or me," for Iaccocca had made a lot of money for Ford.

Henry II was married three times and went through two ugly divorces that fueled the fires of tabloid journalism for several years.

He was also a great philanthropist, and with the help of other public-spirited citizens like Max Fisher, he spearheaded a campaign to revitalize the downtown area of Detroit. A permanent memorial to this tremendous undertaking is the

* from Peter Collier & David Horowitz, *The Fords: An American Epic* (Summit, 1987, $22.95), p. 257.

Detroit Renaissance Center (an office building, convention center, and shopping center), which probably never would have happened without Henry II.

There were many unusual challenges that faced the Ford Motor Company during Henry II's reign as chairman. There were some triumphs, such as the revitalization of Ford's European market, which literally saved the company during the early eighties when Ford misjudged the seriousness of the Arab oil embargo and America's desire for fuel-efficient small cars.

- There was the domination of the small sportscar market by the legendary Mustang.
- The success of the company under various Henry Ford CEO appointees such as Iaccocca, Caldwell, Breech, and currently the tremendous success of the Petersen/Poling team was a testimonial to his ability to select competent people.
- Of course, the ill-fated and -timed Edsel was announced during Henry II's reign. In defense of the Edsel (which has since become a metaphor for monstrous failures), it was a good car that came into a disappearing niche in the marketplace. It was one of the most flagrant screw-ups in market feasibility research in modern history.

When Henry II took over the ailing company in 1945, it prompted one observer to say, "The company is not only dying, but is already dead waiting for rigor mortis to set in."

Help for the fledgling CEO and his ailing company came from an extremely unpredictable and nontraditional source.

The Whiz Kids

In October of 1945, *Life* magazine ran a feature story on Henry II, describing the young CEO as possessing "blunt frankness and intolerance of pretense."*

The article was read by Arjay Miller, a young Army Air Force officer looking for a job. Miller was not just another World War II veteran looking for a civilian job. He was one of a group of ten young Air Force officers "who had developed particular planning and financial skills during the war, and who had decided to stick together and hire themselves out, in peacetime, as a ready-made management team. The team's track record, having served together in the Office of Statistical Control, was outstanding in cost analysis, price control, and management skills; information which was necessary for many of the major strategic

* Lacey, p. 421.

moves by top command. The head of the team, the legendary Charles Thornton, fired off a no-nonsense telegram to Henry Ford saying, 'We have a matter of management importance to discuss with you.' Henry Ford II wasted no time in inviting the entire team to Detroit for a meeting. They were awed by the magnitude of the plant, especially "the great looming mass of the Rouge."*

"What impressed them the most, however—and this was the same for all of the group—was Henry Ford II. He was 'a gleaming figure,' remembered Charles Thornton, 'a young man with determination.' "** He was about the same age as the team. He could not match them in terms of brainpower, but when he entered the room, one against ten, and started talking, this self-assured brain trust began to feel a little less cocky. One member of the team described Henry: "There was something heroic about him, the way he held himself, with his crew cut. He was so upright, so erect. We sensed sincerity in him, something genuine."*** The team had other offers in private industry, but they were so taken with Henry II that all agreed to go to work at Ford.

The Whiz Kids have been popularly credited with the remarkable revival of Ford following World War II, and their success was a testimonial to the young Henry as a leader. "By the time all ten members of the team had completed their business careers, six had become Ford vice-presidents, two had served as president of the company, three had taken CEO jobs in other companies, one held cabinet office—and one had dreamed up a car called the Edsel."****

Ford Goes Public

Because of Henry I's will, in which he left 95 percent of the Ford stock to a foundation in order to beat inheritance taxes, and only the remaining 5 percent to his heirs, a serious cash-flow problem surfaced for the Ford heirs following World War II. The Fords were accustomed to a grand and expensive lifestyle with expensive homes and servants, and the company was not generating nearly enough money in the form of personal dividends to support this mode of living. The Ford Foundation, established by Henry I as an inheritance tax dodge, was garnering most of the dividend income. Also, the regeneration of the company under Ernest Breech was requiring a great deal more capital.

"The obvious solution was to take the company public—to sell its stock on

* Ibid.
** Lacey, p. 421.
*** Ibid.
**** Ibid., p. 422.

the open market. Not only did the family's needs mandate this: The needs of the company itself, the enormous expenses involved in building new factories and keeping the existing operation healthy, meant it could not be run as it had been in the founder's day, like a small grocery store, out of its own cash box. The company's size and prestige demanded that it be listed on the New York Stock Exchange, but the NYSE would not list a nonvoting stock. Somehow there would have to be a plan that would not only satisfy the New York Stock Exchange but also the Ford family, the Ford Foundation, and the ever-watchful IRS. Secrecy was critical, for this was the touchiest deal imaginable, and if word slipped out, there might be considerable opposition to what the Ford family was trying to do."*

It took the investment firm of Goldman Sachs three stress-filled years to complete the offering, which gave the family 40 percent of the voting stock, and a larger share of the equity in the company. There was a frenzy among investors to buy the newly offered stock, and observers commented it was a landmark in the history of public ownership. "It was a landmark in tax avoidance too; estimates were that Eleanor Clay Ford and her four children saved some $300 million in taxes while keeping control of the company."**

Henry II's turbulent life ended on September 29, 1987 from pneumonia. He had served as Ford's CEO from 1945 until October 1, 1979 and retired from the company as an officer and employee in 1982.

Benson Ford's career was bland and colorless, as he held responsible positions principally in the administrative part of the company. He died of a heart attack in July of 1978.

William Clay Ford, the "kid brother," probably never had a chance to realize his full potential because of the timing of his older brother Henry's rise to power. He went to work for the company in 1949. He was chairman of the executive committee in 1978 and was elected vice-chairman of the board of directors in 1980. Bill Ford's destiny was touched by the same dynamics that destroyed the Edsel. He had spearheaded the marketing of a car to go head to head with GM's Cadillac, called the Continental. Unfortunately, the year was 1956 and America was heading into a recession that severely curtailed the luxury car market for the Continental.

After painful physical problems with two ruptured Achilles tendons, coupled with the failure of his Continental in the Ford model line-up, his spirit was broken. "The family drama involving the isolation of Benson and William

* Halberstam, p. 225.
** Halberstam, p. 227.

reached its denouement. Both of them now watched happenings at Ford from the sidelines, a drink in their hands as they slid toward alcoholism."*

One afternoon soon after the Continental was killed, Benson and William were visiting Eleanor, their mother. During the visit she asked them both why they weren't being of more help to Henry. Bill looked at Benson and smiled bitterly. "Because he doesn't want us to, if you really want to know the truth," he said.

William Clay Ford currently owns the Detroit Lions football team.

The Fords of the Future

The prospects for the continuation of the Ford family's involvement in the Ford Motor Company are indeed bright. Not only are the Fords prolific in producing offspring but they have a penchant for producing heirs interested in the automobile business.

Edsel Ford II (Henry II's son), age forty-two, is a member of Ford's board of directors and executive director of the marketing staff. He has worked for the company since 1974 in several management capacities, just completing a hitch as general sales manager of the Lincoln-Mercury division. He has three sons, Henry III, Calvin, and Stewart.

William Clay Ford, Jr., age thirty-three, is also a member of the board of directors. He joined the company in 1979 and has also successfully held several management positions at Ford. His most recent position was Heavy Truck Engineering and Manufacturing manager from July 1989 to March 1990, when he assumed his present position as Director of Business Strategy, Ford Automotive Group. He has two daughters, Eleanor and Alexandra.

Benson Ford, Jr., age forty-one, joined the company in 1986 as a service management specialist, in the Parts and Service Division. He currently is an accessories merchandising specialist in the same division.

Walter Buhl Ford III (son of Josephine Clay Ford), age forty-seven, joined the company in 1978 as program coordinator in the design center. He now is Sales Promotion Coordinator, Lincoln-Mercury Division. He has four children, Bridget, Lindsey, Wendy, and Barbara.

It is more than 100 years since Henry I sold his first automobile for $200 and immediately used the money to build another one. The Ford Motor Company is

* Collier & Horowitz, p. 270.

currently one of the most successful automobile corporations in the world, with revenues in the billions. Like the logo on Ford products, Ford family members in the business are still prominent.

The Ford family has not been immune to tragedy and conflict, but then neither is any family. The unique message from the Fords is their negative family processes did not destroy their family business. Even though many of the Ford clan led colorful and indulgent personal lives, the successful operation of the business was a high priority to most of them.

Appendix I: The Entrepreneur

No business ever started big or by itself. All businesses were launched by entrepreneurs, and all were once small.

You may not know the name William Durant, but he started and twice in his lifetime owned the biggest business in the world, General Motors. Willie was a classic entrepreneur and for many years his persona hung over General Motors. In fact, he once thought to call it Universal Motors and had to change the name because of a possible conflict with another business. To some degree, even today, William Durant affects General Motors.

The most successful business in the world, and by some standards the largest, was started and managed by Tom Watson, Sr. and then his son Tom Watson, Jr. It's not thought of as a family business, probably never was, but a father–son team ran it for fifty-seven years. It is best known today only by its initials, IBM, but it was called International Business Machines when it started in the business of tabulating paper cards. The story told by Tom Watson, Jr. in the recently published *Father, Son & Co., My Life with IBM and Beyond* (Bantam, 1990), is actually a family business story.

Even with these giants, IBM and General Motors, the personality of the entrepreneur as founder hangs over the ongoing business like the smog settling into the Los Angeles basin. It's everywhere, always there, and hard to grasp. To understand a family business, one must begin by understanding the founder, whether dead or alive. Consequently we begin this appendix with a look at the well-accepted information on who is the entrepreneur and what makes him or her tick. It's the beginning of knowledge about the business.

And for the siblings of entrepreneurs, they can also check their profile against our Entrepreneur's Quiz, because there is no law that says you can't have the traits occur father/son, father/son, mother/daughter, mother/daughter, or vice versa. People like Donald Trump, Fred Smith (Federal Express), and Howard Hughes all started their own businesses. All were sons of very successful entrepreneurial fathers. So who is this creature called the entrepreneur?

WHO IS THE ENTREPRENEUR?

Industrial empires were created by great entrepreneurs. To create a business from nothing—and to succeed at it—requires motivation and perseverance bordering on obsession. It sometimes requires ruthlessness. It has nearly always meant neglecting your family and taking long absences from home. All of this could be easily interpreted as antisocial behavior, and none of it is good for a person's reputation. Yet an entrepreneur does all of this and more.

The Early Development of Entrepreneurs

As early as age four or five, entrepreneurs-to-be are peddling lemonade on the sidewalk at a penny a glass. At eight or nine, they're delivering newspapers to earn money for a new bike. In their early teens, they like to collect coins or rocks or stamps or photographs. These activities may be fun, but they are always aimed toward profit and growth. By the time they reach high school they actually may be running their own businesses—on a small scale, of course. In short, most entrepreneurs were enterprising children who had their courses already set toward future enterprises.

The firstborn child is the most likely to become an entrepreneur. Vance Packard, in an article entitled, "The First, Last, and Middle Child: The Surprising Difference,"* highlights various studies (especially one by behavioral scientist Dr. Stanley Schact) that show that firstborns far outnumber later-born children in almost every ranking of achievement. Firstborn children are overly represented in *Who's Who* and they virtually dominate most achievement rankings in United States culture. George Washington, Abraham Lincoln, Thomas Jefferson, Woodrow Wilson, Franklin D. Roosevelt—all were firstborn children. Of the first twenty-three astronauts to go on U.S. space missions, twenty-one

* Vance Packard, "The First, Last, or Middle Child: The Surprising Difference," *Reader's Digest*, December 1969.

were either the oldest or only children. This is remarkable when you consider that later-born children outnumber firstborns by two to one in the general U.S. population. In a recent analysis of 1,618 National Merit Scholarship winners, 971 were firstborn children.

Later in the article, Packard indicates that firstborn children are most likely to accept parents' standards, to be traditionally oriented, and to call themselves religious. It's the later-born who are likely to rebel against the parents' standards. The firstborn tend to be entrepreneurs.

The entrepreneur's obsessive need to achieve may often be traced to his relationship with his father. If they have a "good" relationship—even if Dad was not a great success—the son strives to prove himself and to make Dad proud. Dad's subtlest signs of approval—such as a nod or a half-smile—are the firstborn's most cherished rewards. A surprisingly large number of entrepreneurs are the offspring of self-employed fathers. Thus, many entrepreneurs imitate their fathers and soon become self-employed. The free spirit and the independence of self-employment are molded into many young entrepreneurs-to-be and can never be totally suppressed in their later careers.

In cases where the father–son relationship is less cordial—even strained—the son may be out to "get the old man" by achieving a greater level of success in order to prove he's the better man. Very seldom, it seems, does the entrepreneur ever have what we would consider your average, run-of-the-mill, subdued oedipal relationship with his father.

The above discussion of the entrepreneur's early childhood development uses the pronoun he: Consequently, the female version of this unique person is relegated to a second place. The hard facts have been that starting, financing, and managing a small business have traditionally been men's work: Women had not often chosen this route, but this is changing very rapidly.

Entrepreneurial Traits

One of the initial scholarly studies of entrepreneurship, *The Organization Makers*,* concluded that entrepreneurs had a lower educational base than their counterparts in larger businesses and that often they were not college graduates. This pioneering study of about 100 small businessmen in Michigan indicated that 20 percent of the entrepreneurs studied were immigrants to the United States. Moreover, 35 percent were sons of immigrants. Hence, the surprising conclusion was that 55 percent of the entrepreneurs studied in Michigan in the

* O. Collins and D. Moore (Ann Arbor: University of Michigan, 1970).

fifties were either foreign-born or first-generation Americans. About 20 percent of this sample in Michigan were college graduates.

The studies conducted in the sixties by Professor Edward Roberts of the Sloan School at the Massachusetts Institute of Technology characterized the Boston entrepreneur differently from the earlier Michigan study. Roberts was studying the typical entrepreneur who had founded a new technological enterprise along Route 128 in Boston. The difference between the Boston and the Michigan groupings was most evident in the educational attainment and age of the entrepreneur. Roberts concluded the average age was closer to thirty-five years and the average educational attainment of those in the sample was a master's degree.

Alfred North Whitehead once said, "The greatest invention of all is the invention of inventing inventions." If that is the case, the person who introduces an invention to the world—the entrepreneur—must share the greatness. Much has been written about the entrepreneur—his desires, his motivations, and his characteristics—but most of this literature has been the result of deep scientific investigation that, in our opinion, has neglected the "human" side of the issue.

The New Research

During his career, Mancuso has worked directly with hundreds of entrepreneurs in a variety of businesses and industries. He has been their confidant and sounding board. He's shared their failures and successes.

Mancuso says, "I have worked with winners and losers alike, although each time I began a consulting relationship I was confident that I was working with a winner. But of course this was not always the case. If nothing else, my experience has taught me that it is nearly impossible to predict what makes a 'successful' entrepreneur. It is a good deal easier to predict what causes an entrepreneur to fail."

He continues, "These conclusions about entrepreneurial motivation are mine alone. They are not based on any sensible sampling or interviewing, nor are they based on any statistical fact-gathering. You might call these opinions my 'gut' reaction after working hand-in-glove with so many different entrepreneurs."

Mancuso's research concluded the average age of the entrepreneur to be between thirty and thirty-five years, and that this age was slowly moving down toward a thirty-year-old average. In fact, a good many of the entrepreneurs he studied and worked with actually started their businesses while in their middle or late twenties. More than half the group he studied held a master's degree in either business or a technical discipline.

This does not mean these individuals were brilliant students. In fact, the opposite might well be the case. It does, however, indicate a certain level of respect for education. For some unexplainable reason, the master's degree is the most popular terminal degree, at least for the New England entrepreneur.

"The entrepreneurs I worked with were overwhelmingly the firstborn children of self-employed fathers," says Mancuso. "They were holders of the master's degree and were married when they started their businesses in their early thirties. However, many business men and women also hold master's degrees; and, in their middle thirties, they are working for someone else. These business executives have no business of their own—nor do they have a desire to have one. They are perfectly content with the role of the (hired hand) employee. So, possessing this unusual set of individual characteristics is not enough to be labeled an entrepreneur. In fact, most individuals who possess the unusual grouping of characteristics are not entrepreneurs; rather, they are successful business executives employed in American industry. An entrepreneur must also have the energy, enthusiasm, and positive mental attitude that create the burning inner desire to be your own boss. You've got to be able to go twenty-five hours a day if need be to make the business work—and that takes energy. If you don't have it, all the Wheaties, Ovaltine, and little blue pills in the world aren't going to help."

And just having the magic set of personal characteristics is not enough to be classified as an entrepreneur, either. Just as the earlier research into leadership eventually concluded there was no simple set of personal characteristics that assured leadership ability, the same is true of entrepreneurs. Possessing the traits does not make one an entrepreneur, for this chicken-and-egg question begins with the finding that existing, not aspiring, entrepreneurs have these traits. Only a deep-seated inner drive to start a business from nothing can classify a person as a bonafide entrepreneur. And, as yet, all of the research has failed to uncover the primary sources of motivation prompting a human being to found a new business enterprise.

Entrepreneurial Characteristics

Mancuso often invited outside guests to speak to the college students in the course he taught in entrepreneurship and venture management at Worcester Polytechnic Institute. His purpose was to expose the students to a broader view of the entrepreneurial universe. One of these speakers, Anthony "Spag" Borgatti, founder of Spag's Department Store, one of New England's leading discount centers in Shrewsbury, Massachusetts, is an excellent example of the entrepreneur as an individualist. Every year Spag told the students: "A small business is not an institution. It's a way of life, and the best teacher of life is personal experience. There is no book: You sort of observe and make your own way." In another incident, atter the course was completed, one of the students came to Mancuso and said, "I've listened to every one of our guest speakers—successful and unsuccessful—but I can't figure out the pattern for success. Each speaker was so different." As soon as the student completed his sentence, he realized that he had just answered his own question.

Besides being strong individualists, every entrepreneur is a born optimist. To them the bucket is never half-empty but always half-full. This trait sometimes goes so far that it becomes an unrealistic perspective. However, it takes this kind of undying optimism to survive the false starts, near-failures, and disappointments that every entrepreneur faces every day. They seek out opportunities—and when they don't exist, they create them. Entrepreneurism is an synonym for optimism. Employees of entrepreneurs should keep these basic and fundamental entrepreneurial characteristics in mind in their day-to-day work. Instead of bringing the entrepreneur/boss problems for resolution, bring him opportunities for his consideration. Entrepreneurs have enough problems of their own!

Contrary to popular belief, entrepreneurs are not big gamblers or "high rollers." Although they are unwilling to gamble on long shots, they are more willing to take a chance if their individual skills can affect the probability of success. They love to bet a few dollars on a hole of golf or to wager on a tennis match. These risks involve their skill and they aren't beyond overestimating their abilities—not by a long shot.

Every student of entrepreneurship has, at one time or another, speculated about what motivates a person to leave a good job and security to start his own business. Some say they are basically insecure and must prove their worth on their own. Some say that they just can't work for someone else, that they have to be their own bosses. Others claim they are bored by the slow pace in a large company and hunger for more action. It has even been suggested that they are motivated by a nagging spouse or by the desire to keep up with the Joneses.

Any or all of these factors may influence an entrepreneur's decision to strike out on his own, but more often than not, it is the realization that as long as he is working for someone else, his employer is earning at least 25 percent more than he is paying. Why, asks the entrepreneur, shouldn't he be getting all he is worth?

But don't be misled. It's not the money they are interested in as much as the autonomy of deciding how to allocate their worth. Money, in fact, is a poor reason to go into business, and is probably the reason behind most of the failures. Deciding to go into business solely to make money is a mistake. Most successful companies are founded by someone with an idea and a dream. Making money and accumulating wealth are usually the by-products of accomplishing some nobler goal. You need an idea or a dream to provide the push for success.

There is another personal characteristic that can make or break an entrepreneur, given all the other factors: his or her spouse. If venture capitalists could get to know every client's spouse, they'd have a far better indication of the client's likelihood of success.

Mancuso has toyed with various methods of displaying a spouse's value to a small firm on a balance sheet. He says, "I would rank them right below cash when they're an asset, and just below trade payables when they're a liability.

"It isn't easy being married to an entrepreneur. Living with insecurity and change (often for years), and putting up with broken dates, forgotten birthdays, burned dinners, deep depressions, and a multitude of other hardships. But show me an entrepreneur whose spouse is content and willing to help the entrepreneur, and—much more often than not—I'll show you success."

Management Style

In managing any business enterprise, a delicate balance exists between delegating and abdicating. It is a problem that plagues all businesspeople in both profit and nonprofit enterprises. Entrepreneurs accomplish most tasks better and faster than their employees. It stands to reason: They have all the facts and resources at their disposal, and they also have the authority, so there's no need to communicate with others in order to resolve the problem. They know what to do, so they just do it—and they do it at least three times faster and better. Hence, the issue of delegating is even more difficult in an entrepreneurial for-profit venture.

Sometimes all of this knowledge and authority vested in one person is bad—or at least not all good. Management theory teaches that authority and responsibility should always be in harmony. Yet there is often a serious imbalance between them in a small business. With all of this power vested in one person, the individual often tends to be in a hurry: to decide and do rather than to think, plan, and delegate. Given a choice between doing and thinking, an entrepreneur almost always chooses to do. This is one of the causes of an entrepreneur's managerial ineffectiveness. They are poor delegators. Graphically stated, where most people would say "Ready, aim, fire!" the entrepreneur impatiently shouts, "Ready, fire, aim!"

Entrepreneurs have difficulty in managing people. They have neither the patience nor the inclination to get down to the nitty-gritty of motivating an employee to perform. Perhaps it's because they tend to be more creative. Perhaps they're too self-centered. Maybe they're even too busy to properly address the issues in successorship planning. Whatever the reason, they're not good at delegating or teaching, and when they do give power to a subordinate or a successor candidate, they usually abdicate and become totally uninvolved—unless they have to jump back in to put out fires!

Heroes

Nearly every profession has its heroes. Visit any graduate school of law and you'll find portraits of Daniel Webster, Clarence Darrow, and other luminaries of the legal profession hanging in the halls. In the medical schools there are bound to be portraits of Hippocrates, Pasteur, or Paul Dudley White. These men are the universal heroes of their professions.

Do you know the name of the president of General Motors, General Foods, General Electric, or General Mills? I'll give you a hint: None of them are generals. In business, there are no universal heroes. The presidents of the biggest U.S. corporations are uncelebrated and unknown. The only portraits on the business school walls are those of the faculty.

Heroes in business are personal heroes. Nearly every entrepreneur has one—a person whose career they have followed, a person whom they admire and try to emulate. Discover the identity of an entrepreneur's heroes and you'll learn a lot about them. Their ability to follow or parrot an inspiring person or message is unusual. Entrepreneurs understand their self-defined mission, and these heroes are often instrumental during the pursuit of the chosen destiny.

During the upward climb from a small business to a bigger enterprise, the style and manner of thinking of the entrepreneur's hero often plays a subconscious role. When an entrepreneur is backed into a corner and has no answer, he'll often muse, "What would so-and-so do in this case?" During the upward climb, the entrepreneur often suffers from great exhilarations and depressions. The upward struggle is so energy-sapping that it creates unusual personality traits within normal would-be entrepreneurs.

Hunches

One weakness many entrepreneurs are prone to is the tendency to "fall in love" too easily: They go wild over new employees, products, suppliers, machines, and methods. Anything new excites them. These "love affairs" usually don't last long; many are over as suddenly as they begin, rather like a sudden summer shower. The problem is that during these affairs, the entrepreneur may alienate some people, be stubborn about listening to opposite views, and lose his objectivity. It's a dangerous trait if it's practiced with intense passion. A good medicine for this disease is to spend a few moments a day recalling past infatuations. While you're daydreaming about your past love affairs, extend the practice to old-fashioned daydreaming about anything at all. You see, daydreaming isn't all bad, as it tends to sharpen your subconscious ideas and, in turn, stimulate your hunches.

This tendency to be intuitive is not all bad, however. The process of guessing right and betting on hunches is a positive feature known as the entrepreneur's intuition. Rather than destroying the sensations of pursuing novel problem-solving methods, a wiser entrepreneur would only seek to control or modify his intuitive impulses. A careful program of checks and balances—monitored by a good financial officer or an active board of directors—can accomplish this objective. Ignoring the intuition could relegate one of the positive features of entrepreneurs to a neutral status. The controlling mechanism takes some prior planning to get in place, but better an ounce of prevention than a pound of cure. Organizing to capitalize on intuitive hunches while avoiding false love affairs is a trait well worth acquiring.

What makes an entrepreneur run? Why is he more at home in his swivel chair than in his living room? Why can't she be happy working for someone else? Why does he always have to go it alone? What's with him anyway? When the other kids were out playing ball, why was she busy hustling lemonade? When his friends were dating cheerleaders, why was he organizing rock concerts? Or marketing grandmother's pickle recipe? Or inventing a better fly swatter? Is he really smarter than the rest of us? Or just crazy?

What Mancuso concluded during his research was that, strangely enough, entrepreneurs do share many traits—too many to be purely coincidental. And, when he started to dig deeper, he hit on all kinds of weird phenomena.

THE ENTREPRENEUR'S QUIZ

Who is the entrepreneur? What molds him and what motivates him? How does he differ from the nine-to-fiver, and where are those differences most telling? Why will one brother set out to build a business while another aspires to promotions and perks? Why does one stay up nights working on a business plan while the other brags about his pension plan? Is it brains? Luck? Hard work? Or does it just happen?

The entrepreneur represents freedom: Freedom from the boss, freedom from the time clock, and, with a lot of hard work and more than a little luck, freedom from the bank.

Entrepreneurs are the backbone of the free enterprise system. When an entrepreneur gambles on his skills and abilities, everyone stands to win. New and innovative products and services created by entrepreneurs constantly revitalize the marketplace and create thousands of new jobs in the process. What's more, nothing keeps a big corporation on its toes like an entrepreneur nipping at its heels—and its markets.

So who is the entrepreneur? Anyone who's ever looked at a problem and seen an opportunity as well as a solution is a likely prospect. The same goes for anyone who feels his ambition is being held in check by corporate red tape. But it takes more than just cleverness and frustration to get an entrepreneurial venture off the ground. It takes guts, an indefatigable personality, and nothing short of a total dedication to a dream. On top of that, it takes the kind of person who can call working ninety hours a week fun.

While there is no single entrepreneurial archetype, there are certain character traits that indicate an entrepreneurial personality. In this quiz, we've tried to concentrate on those indicators. If you've ever wondered if you have what it takes to be an entrepreneur, here is your chance to find out.

Quiz

1. How were your parents employed?
   a. Both worked and were self-employed for most of their working lives.
   b. Both worked and were self-employed for some part of their working lives.
   c. One parent was self-employed for most of his or her working life.
   d. One parent was self-employed at some point in his or her working life.
   e. Neither parent was ever self-employed.
2. Have you ever been fired from a job?
   a. Yes, more than once.
   b. Yes, once.
   c. No.
3. Are you an immigrant, or were your parents or grandparents immigrants?
   a. I was born outside the United States.
   b. One or both of my parents were born outside the United States.
   c. At least one of my grandparents was born outside of the United States.
   d. Does not apply.
4. Your work career has been:
   a. Primarily in small business (under 100 employees).
   b. Primarily in medium-sized business (100–500 employees).
   c. Primarily in big business (over 500 employees).
5. Did you operate any businesses before you were twenty?
   a. Many.
   b. A few.
   c. None.

6. What is your present age?
   a. 21–30
   b. 31–40
   c. 41–50
   d. 51 or over.

7. Your highest level of formal education is:
   a. Some high school.
   b. High school diploma.
   c. Bachelor's degree.
   d. Master's degree.
   e. Doctorate.

8. What would be your primary motivation in starting a business?
   a. To make money.
   b. I don't like working for someone else.
   c. To be famous.
   d. As an outlet for excess energy.

9. Your relationship to the parent who provided most of the family's income was:
   a. Strained.
   b. Comfortable.
   c. Competitive.
   d. Nonexistent.

10. You find the answers to difficult questions by:
    a. Working hard.
    b. Working smart.
    c. Both.

11. On whom do you rely for critical management advice?
    a. Internal management teams.
    b. External management professionals.
    c. External financial professionals.
    d. No one except myself.

12. If you were at the racetrack, which of these would you bet on?
    a. The daily double—a chance to make a killing.
    b. A 10-to-1 shot.
    c. A 3-to-1 shot.
    d. The 2-to-1 favorite.

13. The only ingredient that is both necessary and sufficient for starting a business is:
    a. Money.
    b. Customers.
    c. An idea or product.
    d. Motivation and hard work.

14. At a cocktail party, you:
    a. Are the life of the party.
    b. Never know what to say to people.
    c. Just fit into the crowd.
    d. You never go to cocktail parties.

15. You tend to "fall in love" too quickly with:
    a. New product ideas.
    b. New employees.
    c. New manufacturing ideas.
    d. New financial plans.
    e. All of the above.

16. Which of the following personality types is best suited to be your right-hand person?
    a. Bright and energetic.
    b. Bright and lazy.
    c. Dumb and energetic.
    d. Dumb and lazy.

17. You accomplish tasks better because:
    a. You are always on time.
    b. You are super-organized.
    c. You keep good records.
    d. All of the above.

18. You hate to discuss:
    a. Problems involving employees.
    b. Signing expense accounts.
    c. New management practices.
    d. The future of the business.

19. Given a choice, you would prefer:
    a. Rolling dice with a 1-in-3 chance of winning.
    b. Working on a problem with a 1-in-3 chance of solving it in the time allocated.

20. If you could choose between the following competitive professions, your choice would be:
    a. Professional golf.
    b. Sales.
    c. Personnel counseling.
    d. Teaching.

21. If you had to choose between working with a partner who is a close friend and working with a stranger who is an expert in your field, you would choose:
    a. The close friend.
    b. The expert.

22. In business situations that demand action, clarifying who is in charge will help produce results. Do you
    a. Agree.
    b. Agree, with reservations.
    c. Disagree.

23. In playing a competitive game, you are concerned with:
    a. How well you play.
    b. Winning or losing.
    c. Both of the above.
    d. Neither of the above.

Scoring

1. (a) 10
   (b) 5
   (c) 5
   (d) 2
   (e) 0

2. (a) 10
   (b) 7
   (c) 0

3. (a) 5
   (b) 4
   (c) 3
   (d) 0

4. (a) 10
   (b) 5
   (c) 0

5. (a) 10
   (b) 7
   (c) 0

6. (a) 8
   (b) 10
   (c) 5
   (d) 2

7. (a) 2
   (b) 3
   (c) 10
   (d) 8
   (e) 4

8. (a) 0
   (b) 15
   (c) 0
   (d) 0

9. (a) 10
   (b) 5
   (c) 10
   (d) 5

10. (a) 0
    (b) 5
    (c) 10

11. (a) 0
    (b) 10
    (c) 0
    (d) 5

12. (a) 0
    (b) 2
    (c) 10
    (d) 3

	(a)	(b)	(c)	(d)	(e)
13.	0	10	0	0	
14.	0	10	3	0	
15.	5	5	5	5	15
16.	2	10	0	0	
17.	15	15	5	15	
18.	8	10	0	0	
19.	0	15			
20.	3	10	0	0	
21.	0	10			
22.	10	2	0		
23.	8	10	15	0	

1. It's only natural that a child who has grown up in a home where at least one parent is self-employed is more likely to try his hand at his own business than a child whose parents were in, say, government service. Some good examples of this are Howard Hughes, Fred Smith of Federal Express, and New York real estate tycoon Donald Trump, all of whom parlayed modest family businesses into major fortunes.

2. Steven Jobs and Steven Wozniak went ahead with Apple Computers when their project was rejected by their respective employers, Atari and Hewlett-Packard. When Thomas Watson was fired by National Cash Register in 1913, he joined up with the Computer-Tabulating-Recording Company and ran it until a month before his death in 1956. He also changed the company's name to IBM.

3. America is still the land of opportunity and a hotbed for entrepreneurship. The displaced people who arrive on our shores (and at our airports) every day, be they Cuban, Korean, or Vietnamese, can still turn hard work and enthusiasm into successful business enterprises. Though it is far from a necessary ingredient for entrepreneurship, the need to succeed is often greater among those whose backgrounds contain an extra struggle to fit into society.

4. I've heard it said that "inside every corporate body there's an entrepreneur struggling to escape." However, small business management is more than just a scaled-down version of big business management. Whereas the professional manager is skilled at protecting resources, the entrepreneurial manager is skilled at creating them. An entrepreneur is at his best when he can still control all aspects of his company. That's why so many successful entrepreneurs have been kicked out of the top spot when their companies outgrew their talents (Steven Jobs).

5. The enterprising adult first appears as the enterprising child. Coin and stamp collecting, mowing lawns, shoveling snow, promoting dances and rock concerts—all are common examples of early business ventures. The paper route of today could be the Federal Express of tomorrow.

6. The average age of entrepreneurs has been steadily shifting downward since the late fifties and sixties when it was found to be between forty and forty-five. Our most recent research puts the highest concentration of entrepreneurs in their thirties, but people like Jobs and Wozniak of Apple Computers, Ed DeCastro and Herb Richman of Data General, and Fred Smith of Federal Express all got their business off the ground while still in their twenties. Although we look for this data to stabilize right around thirty, there are always exceptions. Computer whiz Jonathan Rotenberg is just such an exception. In 1978, Rotenberg's advice was solicited by the promoter of an upcoming public computer show. After conferring several times on the phone, the promoter suggested they meet for a drink to continue their discussion. "I can't," Rotenberg replied. When asked, "Why not?" Jonathan answered, "Because I'm only fifteen."

7. The question of formal education among entrepreneurs has always been controversial. Studies have shown that many entrepreneurs, like W. Clement Stone, had failed to finish high school, not to mention college. And Polaroid's founder Edwin Land has long been held up as an example of an "entrepreneur in a hurry" because he dropped out of Harvard in his freshman year to get his business off the ground.

However, our data concludes that the most common educational level achieved by entrepreneurs is the bachelor's degree, and the trend seems headed toward the master's degree. However, few entrepreneurs have the time or patience to earn a doctorate. Notable exceptions include Robert Noyce and Gordon Moore of Intel, An Wang of Wang Laboratories, and Robert Collings of Data Terminal Systems.

8. Entrepreneurs don't like working for anyone but themselves. While money is always a consideration, there are easier ways to make money than by going it alone. More often than not, money is a by-product (albeit a welcome one) of an entrepreneur's motivation rather than the motivation itself.

9. Past studies have always emphasized the strained or competitive relationship between the entrepreneur and the income-producing parent (usually the father). The entrepreneur has traditionally been out to "pick up the pieces" for the family or to "show the old man," while at the same time always seeking his grudging praise.

However, our study showed a surprising percentage of the entrepreneurs had what they considered to be comfortable relationships with their income-producing parents. We think it's directly related to the changing ages and educational backgrounds of the new entrepreneurs. The new entrepreneurs are children of the sixties, not the children of the Depression. In most cases they're college-educated. The entrepreneur's innate independence has not come into such dramatic conflict with the father as it might have in the past. Mancuso still feels that a strained or competitive relationship best fits the entrepreneurial profile, though the nature of this relationship is no longer black and white.

10. The difference between the hard worker and the smart worker is the difference between the hired hand and the boss. What's more, the entrepreneur usually enjoys what he's doing so much that he rarely notices how hard he's really working. Mancuso says, "A decision is an action taken by an executive when the information he has is so incomplete that the answer doesn't suggest itself. The entrepreneur's job is to make sure the answers always suggest themselves."

11. Entrepreneurs seldom rely on internal people for major policy decisions because employees very often have pet projects to protect or personal axes to grind. What's more, internal management people will seldom offer conflicting opinions on big decisions, and in the end the entrepreneur makes the decision on his own.

Outside financial sources are also infrequent sounding boards when it comes to big decisions because they simply lack the imagination that characterizes most entrepreneurs. The most noble ambition of most bankers and accountants is to maintain the status quo.

When it comes to critical decisions, entrepreneurs most often rely on outside management consultants and other entrepreneurs. In fact, Mancuso's follow-up work has shown that outside management professionals have played a role in *every* successful business he studied, which wasn't the case in unsuccessful ventures.

12. Contrary to popular belief, entrepreneurs are not high risk-takers. They tend to set realistic and achievable goals, and when they do take risks, they're usually calculated. If an entrepreneur found himself in Atlantic City with just ten dollars in his pocket, chances are he'd spend it on telephone calls and not on slot machines.

13. All business begins with orders, and orders can only come from customers. You might think you're in business when you've developed a prototype or after you've raised capital, but bankers and venture capitalists only buy potential. It takes customers to buy products.

14. The entrepreneur is a very social person and often a very charming person. (Remember, an entrepreneur is someone who gets things done, and getting things done often involves charming the right banker or supplier.) And while he will often only talk about things concerning himself or his business, his enthusiasm is such that anything he talks about sounds interesting.

15. One of the biggest weaknesses that entrepreneurs face is their tendency to "fall in love" too easily. They go wild over new employees, products, suppliers, machines, methods, and financial plans. Anything new excites them. But these "love affairs" usually don't last long; many of them are over as suddenly as they begin. The problem is that during these affairs entrepreneurs can quite easily alienate their staffs, become stubborn about listening to opposing views, and lose their objectivity.

16. The "bright and lazy" personality makes the best assistant. He's not out to prove himself, so he won't be butting heads with the entrepreneur at every turn. He's relieved at not having to make critical decisions, but he's a whiz at implementing those made by others. Unlike the entrepreneur, he's good at delegating responsibilities. Getting others to do the work for him is his specialty!

17. Organization is the key to an entrepreneur's success. Organizational systems may differ, but you'll never find an entrepreneur who's without one. Some keep lists on their desks, always crossing things off from the top and adding to the bottom.

18. The only thing an entrepreneur likes less than discussing employee problems is discussing petty cash slips and expense accounts. Solving problems is what an entrepreneur does best. What entrepreneurs want to know is how much their salespeople are selling, not how much they're padding their expense accounts.

19. Entrepreneurs are optimists and believe that with the right amount of time and money, they can do anything.

Chance certainly plays a part in anyone's career—being in the right place at the right time—but entrepreneurs have a tendency to make their own chances. There is the story of the shoe manufacturer who sent his two sons to the Mediterranean to scout out new markets. One wired back: "No point in staying on. No one here wears shoes." The other son wired back: "Terrific opportunities. Thousands still without shoes." Who do you think eventually took over the business?

20. Sales gives instant feedback on your performance; it's the easiest job of all for measuring success. How do personnel counselors or teachers ever know if they're winning or losing? Entrepreneurs need immediate feedback and are always capable of adjusting their strategies in order to win.

21. The best thing an entrepreneur can do for a friendship is to spare it the extra strain of a working relationship. By carefully dividing their work lives and their social lives, the entrepreneur insures that business decisions will always be in the best interests of the business.

22. Everyone knows that a camel is a horse that was designed by a committee, and unless it's clear that one person is in charge, decisions are bound to suffer from a committee mentality.

23. Vince Lombardi is famous for saying, "Winning isn't everything, it's the only thing," but a lesser-known quote of his is closer to the entrepreneur's philosophy. Looking back at a season, Lombardi was heard to remark, "We didn't lose any games last season, we just ran out of time twice."

Entrepreneuring is a competitive game and an entrepreneur has to be prepared to run out of time occasionally. Walt Disney, Henry Ford, and Milton Hershey all experienced bankruptcy before experiencing success. The right answer to this question is (c), but the best answer is the game itself.

Your Entrepreneurial Profile

194–244	Successful Entrepreneur
159–193	Entrepreneur
144–158	Latent Entrepreneur
129–143	Potential Entrepreneur
119–128	Borderline Entrepreneur
Below 118	Hired Hand

Appendix II: Family Business Resources

Contents

Playing to Your Strengths

I wanted to relate a personal story, but I was reluctant to make it a "must read." So I decided to begin the resource section of the book with it. It's a little family concept that took me close to fifty years to master. When I was in my twenties, my oldest child, Karyn Mancuso, had constant trouble in school with mathematics. She had difficulty with fractions and decimals and was always bringing home bad report cards in arithmetic. My wife and I tried to help, but we made little progress. Then my wife decided the best solution was to hire a professional tutor for three afternoons a week. We did this off and on for about five years. It helped as Karyn eventually passed her math exams.

Looking back twenty years, I often recall the "hiring the tutor" process. We must have gone through about forty tutors. They all only lasted a few weeks (some only a few days). We were always running advertisements and interviewing.

We believed neither parent could be both a parent and a math tutor. I think we were correct about that assumption. The good news came when an attractive young woman named Connie Constantino became Karyn's math tutor. Connie had long blond hair and spent half her time in personal grooming. Karyn kept her eyes wide open and picked up every one of the grooming tips, and about 10 percent of the mathematics tips.

Today, Karyn is in her late twenties and she and I often chuckle about her "math tutors." She loved Connie not because she was the best at fractions and decimals, but because she taught Karyn fashion and grooming. Today Karyn is a very well-known aerobics instructor, and her need for mathematical skills are minimal. After all, she says, "I have a calculator and it works just fine."

It never occurred to my wife to hire a tutor in art, fashion, or aerobics for Karyn. We never discussed it even once. I, unfortunately, didn't play a significant decision-making role in this process, only in dutifully interviewing the tutors.

Poor Karyn had to suffer with an excessive emphasis on mathematics, and her natural skills in the arts were seldom encouraged.

Today, if I had the luxury to do it again, I'd have hired Connie to do both arts and mathematics. Sometimes, it pays to play up your child's strengths rather than only propping up her weaknesses. Karyn is married and has a two-year-old daughter (my granddaughter) named Jaeda. I can already observe this blue-eyed redhead excelling at fashion, dance, music, and the arts. Karyn and I agree this shortcoming will not be repeated in her generation.

It's probably only a little point about raising children, and it does not make much difference as to whether or not a family business is involved. But, it occurred to me that the same issue arises in many families; I don't seek to reduce the demand for math tutors—as we all need them—but I'd like to expand the demand for tutors in art, music, dance, fashion, exercise, and so forth.

—Joseph R. Mancuso

ACCOUNTANTS

Below is a select list of accountants competent in family business matters, who are able to handle questions.

Harvey Goldstein
Singer, Lewak,
Greenbaum & Goldstein
10960 Wilshire Blvd.
Suite 826
Los Angeles, CA 90024
(213) 477–3924

Larry Ranallo
Price Waterhouse
600 Grant St., Suite 4500
Pittsburgh, PA 15219
(412) 355–7777

Joseph Murphy
Price Waterhouse
16479 Dallas Pkwy.
Suite 819
Dallas, TX 75248
(214) 733–1212

Keith L. Voights
Peat Marwick Main &
Company
1601 Elm St., Suite 1400
Dallas, TX 75201
(214) 754–2239

Mark Lancaster
Deloitte, Haskins & Sells
1400 Lincoln Plaza
Dallas, TX 75201
(214) 954–4628

Alan S. Zelbow
Miller, Wachman & Co.
40 Broad St.
Boston, MA 02109
(617) 338–6800

Irwin S. Friedman
FER&S
401 North Michigan Ave.
Chicago, IL 60611
(312) 644–6000

Samuel Oliva
Edwin C. Sigel Ltd.
3400 Dundee Rd.,
Suite 180
Northbrook, IL 60062
(708) 291–1333

Richard J. Salute,
Partner
Arthur Andersen &
Company
1345 Ave. of the Americas
New York, NY 10105
(212) 708–3643

Jay W. Trien
Managing Partner
Trien, Rosenberg, Felix,
Rosenberg, Barr &
Weinberg
177 Madison Ave.
Morristown, NJ
07960-6016
(201) 267–4200

Advertising

The most comprehensive source of print media information is the Gale Directory of Newspapers and Periodicals (the former Ayer Directory of Publications).

Gale Research Company
835 Penobscot Building
Detroit, MI 48226
(800) 877–4253

Bacon's Publicity Checker is the finest comprehensive source of publicity information in the United States. This is the source used by most public relations firms. It is published annually; four seasonal supplements list magazines and daily and weekly newspapers in the United States and Canada. Listings include information on circulation, frequency, publication dates, and types of publicity used. The cost is $140.

Bacon's
332 S. Michigan Ave., Suite 900
Chicago, IL 60604
(312) 922–2400
(800) 621–0561

Standard Periodicals Directory is an excellent comprehensive list of periodicals. This service offers eleven separate directories, and gives advertising rates, specifications, and circulation for publications, broadcast stations, and other media.

Patricia Hagood
Oxbridge Communications
150 Fifth Ave., Suite 301
New York, NY 10011
(212) 741–0231

Ulrich's *Directory of Periodicals,* available in most libraries, is also an excellent source.

R. R. Bowker Company
249 W. 17th St.
New York, NY 10011
(212) 645–9700

Standard Rate & Data is an extensive source of both print and eletronic media; it is a classic source of detailed information.

Standard Rate & Data (SRDS)
3004 Glenview Rd.
Wilmette, IL 60091
(708) 256–6067

Internal Publications Directory is an all-in-one directory of house organs. It's a good and unusual method of obtaining publicity.

National Research Bureau
424 N. Third St.
Burlington, IA 52601
(319) 752–5415

Advertising Agencies

Below are some agencies that deal with family business matters. For information:

Michael A. Houle
The Audy Group, Inc.
13321 New Hampshire Ave.
Suite 203
Silver Spring, MD 20904
(301) 236–9496

Devon Blaine
The Blaine Group
7465 Beverly Blvd.
Los Angeles, CA 90036
(213) 938–2577

Carole Marchesano
Goldberg, Marchesano,
Kohlman
927 15th St., N.W.
Washington, DC 20005
(202) 789–2000

Louis J. Cardamone
MARC Advertising
Four Station Square,
Suite 500
Pittsburgh, PA 15219
(415) 562–2000, ext. 2004

Periodicals

Advertising Age, which is published weekly, is the leading newspaper serving the advertising industry. Presented in a tabloid format, issues exceed 100 pages. This widely read and often-quoted paper focuses on advertising in the broadest sense.

Advertising Age
Crain Communications
740 N. Rush St.
Chicago, IL 60611
(312) 649–5200

Adweek publishes five weekly regional editions that report on the advertising industry: Adweek/East, Adweek/Midwest, Adweek/Southeast, Adweek/Southwest, and Adweek/West. Look in your local Yellow Pages or contact the publisher at the address below.

Adweek
ASM Communications
49 E. 21st St.
New York, NY 10010-6213
(212) 529–5500

ARTICLES

Please note: We have provided the address and telephone numbers of those publications listed below that we judged to have articles of interest on family business. We suggest you contact them directly for updates on more current materials.

Business Week. This magazine often runs family business articles and occasionally conducts family business seminars headed by the offspring of famous families.

Business Week
1221 Ave. of the Americas
New York, NY 10020
(212) 512–3896

Teresa Carson, Debra Michaels, and Laurie Baum, "Honey, What Do You Say We Start Our Own Business," September 15, 1986.

Katherine M. Hafner, "Father Knows Best—Just Ask the Tramiel Boys," December 15, 1986.

Stewart Toy, "The New Nepotism," April 4, 1988.

John Byrne, "Braving a Family Run Business," July 11, 1988.

California Business. This is an academic journal which occasionally runs articles on family business.

California Business
4221 Wilshire Blvd.
Suite 400
Los Angeles, CA 90010
(213) 937–5820

Bill Hackman, "Family Ties," April, 1986.

Cosmopolitan. This magazine geared to women often runs stories on the role of the mother or daughter in a business.

Cosmopolitan
224 W. 57th St.
New York, NY 10019
(212) 649–2000

Robert Karen, "Women Who Take Over the Family Business," September, 1987. Six daughters who enter the family business.

The Entrepreneurial Managers Newsletter. This is a monthly publication of the twelve-year-old Center for Entrepreneurial Management Inc. (CEM), a nonprofit membership association of CEOs and entrepreneurs:

The Center for Entrepreneurial Management, Inc.
180 Varick St., Penthouse
New York, NY 10014
(212) 633–0060

Family Feuds—The Gucci Dynasty, January, 1989.

Family Business Impasse, January, 1989.

How to put the family back in family business, May, 1990.

Management succession in family business, June, 1990.

Giving your business to your family, June, 1990.

Family tax breaks: How to share income with your family, September, 1990.

Family Business Magazine. For the past few years, this new magazine has consistently had the best articles on this subject. They are too numerous to list.

Leonard Zweig, Publisher
Steve Solomon, Editor
Family Business Magazine
Rittenhouse Square
229 S. 18th St.
Philadelphia, PA 19103
(215) 790–7000

Forbes Magazine. one of the best-written general business magazines with a strong financial orientation with articles mostly about big business. The Forbes 400 issue lists the richest Americans and has a section on the wealthiest families. The magazine itself is a classic example of a well-run family business. The late legendary entrepreneur Malcolm Forbes left control of the magazine to his oldest son, and left equal asset allocations to his other children. *Family Business* magazine tells the story in its December 1990 issue. Although the articles listed are from 1987, current issues will continue to feature family business.

Forbes Magazine
60 Fifth Ave.
New York, NY 10011
(212) 620–2200

Leonard Burr, "Heir Raising," September 7, 1987.

Edward Cone, "Dad, I Know I Can Handle It," October 26, 1987.

Edward Cone, "Grandson Power," October 26, 1987.

Dyan Machan, "My Partner, My Spouse," December 14, 1987.

Entrepreneurial Woman. This is a new publication of *Entrepreneur* magazine that is beginning to cover the field of women's issues in business.

Entrepreneurial Woman
2392 Morse Ave.
Irvine, CA 92714
(714) 261–2325

Fortune Magazine. This is a bi-weekly business magazine that competes with *Forbes* and *Business Week*. It features stories about families in large businesses.

Fortune Magazine
1271 Ave. of the Americas
New York, NY 10020
(212) 522–1212

Jaclyn Fierman, "How Gallo Crushes the Competition," September 20, 1986. The story of Ernest and Julio Gallo—all the best.

Brett Duval Fromson, "Keeping It All in the Family," September 25, 1989. The story of Jack Daniels bourbon, produced by Brown Forman, a well-known Kentucky distiller that operates the family business with planned nepotism.

Harvard Business Review. The *Review* runs in-depth articles with strong academic analysis components. Under new editor Rosbeth Moss Kanter, it is taking a more "newsy" editorial approach. It is worth obtaining just for the index to other articles.

Harvard Business Review
Soldiers Field
Boston, MA 02163
(617) 495–6800

Manfred Kets DeVries, "The Dark Side of CEO Succession," January–February, 1988.

Thomas Teal and Geraldine Willigan, "The Outstanding Outsider and the Fumbling Family," September–October, 1989.

Inc. This magazine runs frequent stories on family business and occasionally conducts one-day workshops for family business owners. With its circulation of almost 800,000, it reaches most family businesses.

Inc.
38 Commercial Wharf
Boston, MA 02110
(617) 248–8000

Curtis Hartman, "Taking the 'Family' Out of Family Business," September, 1986.

Marshall Paisner, "Myths About Succession," October, 1986.

Bruce Posner, "All My Sons," January, 1987.

Curtis Hartman, "Why Daughters Are Better," August, 1987.

Joshua Hyatt, "Ghost Story: A Struggle Between Father and Son," July, 1988.

Ellen Wojohn, "Share the Wealth/Spoil the Child," August, 1989.

Journal of Small Business Management. This is an academic journal that occasionally features family business articles.

Bureau of Business Research
College of Business
West Virginia University
Morgantown, WV 26506

Radha Changanti, "Management in Women-Owned Enterprises," October, 1986.

Nations Business. We consider this magazine, published by the Chamber of Commerce, to be the single best general interest business magazine. (The new *Family Business Magazine,* published out of Philadelphia, vies for this distinction.) It often features a listing of family business seminars across the country—an excellent resource.

Nations Business
1615 H St., N.W.
Washington, DC 20062
(202) 463–5650

Devins T. Jaffe, "Taking Stock of Your Family Business," February, 1988.

John Ward, "Bringing the Kids into Your Business," February, 1988.

Sharon Nelton, "Fathers and Sons, No Easy Business," February, 1989.

Sharon Nelton, "Marrying into a Family Business," April, 1989.

Benjamin Benson, "Do You Keep Too Many Secrets," August, 1989.

John Ward and Laurel Sorenson, "The Role of Mom," August, 1989.

Sharon Nelton, "Staying Aboard After the Sale," September, 1989.

New York Times. This famous daily newspaper often features well-known families. The May 24th, 1989 issue has an excellent article by Mathew Wald, "Stew Leonard's: Believe it or not."

New York Times
229 W. 43rd St.
New York, NY 10036
(212) 556–1234

Psychology Today. This now-defunct monthly magazine often ran stories on famous families, with a focus on behavioral issues. Check your local library for back issues. For your information, their address was:

Psychology Today
80 Fifth Ave.
New York, NY 10011

Peter Ediden, "Drowning in Wealth," April, 1989 (How to raise rich offspring).

Sales and Marketing Management. A sales magazine that occasionally runs articles on family business.

Sales and Marketing Management
633 Third Ave.
New York, NY 10017
(212) 986–4800

Liz Murphy, "Family Business: Who's Minding the Store," July, 1987.

U.S. News & World Report. A general news magazine that competes with *Time* and *Newsweek.* It sometimes features articles on family enterprises.

U.S. News & World Report
599 Lexington Ave.
New York, NY 10022
(212) 326–5300

Andrea Gabor, "High Stake Family Feuds," February 3, 1986. The story of the families of Getty, Ford, Hearst, Sabastani, and Johnson.

Wall Street Journal. This daily publication often runs excellent series on entrepreneurial families.

Wall Street Journal
World Financial Center
200 Liberty St.
New York, NY 10281
(212) 416–2000

Mark Robichaux, "Business First, Family Second," May 12, 1989.

John B. Emshwilles, "Handing Down the Business," May 19, 1989 (Reasons early succession selection can fail).

Udayab Gupta and Mark Robuchaux, "Reins Tangle Easily at Family Firms," August 9, 1989 (Problems of succession).

Lee Burton, "Inheritance Tax is Choking Successors to Family Firms," August 23, 1989 (The burden of estate tax freeze positions).

George Melloan, "Keeping Things Simple in a Big Family Business," August 29, 1989 (The story of the Jervis B. Webb Company in Michigan).

Working Woman Magazine. A woman's magazine that often runs stories on the role of the mother or daughter in a business.

Working Woman Magazine
342 Madison Ave.
New York, NY 10173
(212) 309-9800

Diane Barthel, "When Husbands and Wives Try to Work Together," November, 1985.

Mattha M. Jablow, "Mixing Family and Business," September, 1986.

Associations/Organizations

Many organizations benefit small businesses and family enterprises in many ways, providing business advice, making contacts, lobbying local, state, and federal governments for favorable legislation.

The Chief Executive Officers Club (CEO Club) is a group of some 350 CEOs who are dedicated to improving the quality and profitability of their companies through shared experience and personal growth. Eight meetings a year are held in each of eight city locations: Boston, New York, Dallas, Chicago, Los Angeles, San Francisco, Washington, DC, and Pittsburgh. This is an elite group of CEOs who run businesses with more than $2 million in annual sales. The CEO Club also sponsors three-day seminar programs: The Management Course for CEOs, the Family Business Experience, and the Power of Persuasion Seminar, which are conducted twice yearly across the United States. The Family Business Experience is not an academic program but a program geared to CEO families seeking to share ideas.

Dr. Joseph Mancuso, President
Chief Executive Officers Clubs
(CEO Clubs)
180 Varick St.,
Penthouse Floor
New York, NY 10014-4606
(212) 633–0060

The Young Presidents Organization is an international group with strong local chapters.

Young Presidents Organization (YPO)
451 S. Becker Dr., Suite 200
Irving, TX 75062
(214) 541–1044

The Executive Committee (also known as TEC) is a California-based association of CEOs meeting in local units across the United States and overseas (Japan). They act as a board of directors for businesses. Meetings are held monthly and annual fees are above $7,000.

Bill Williams
The Executive Committee (TEC)
3737 Camino Del Rio South
Suite 206
San Diego, CA 92108
(619) 563–5875

The National Federation of Independent Business (NFIB) provides a strong voice for small business interests. NFIB also publishes a newsletter, the *NFIB Mandate,* which appears eight times per year. It polls its membership to determine lobbying positions.

John Sloan, President
NFIB
Capitol Gallery East, Suite 700
600 Maryland Ave., S.W.
Washington, DC 20024
(202) 554–9000

The National Small Business United is primarily a lobbying group serving manufacturers, service businesses, retailers, and wholesalers.

John Galles, President
National Small Business United
1155 15th St., N.W.
Suite 710
Washington, DC 20005
(202) 293–8830

The Small Business Legislative Council is a coalition of trade and professional associations that is an effective lobbying group.

John Satagaj
Small Business Legislative Council
1156 15th St., N.W., Suite 510
Washington, DC 20005
(202) 639–8500

The United Shareholders Association (USA) is a political group dedicated to representing shareholders' rights on Capitol Hill.

T. Boone Pickens
United Shareholders Association
1667 K St., N.W., Suite 770
Washington, DC 20006
(202) 393–4600

A group that services high school and young entrepreneurs also does extensive work internationally, including in the Soviet Union. They primarily offer a package of books and tapes to teach the youth of the world to be entrepreneurs.

Nasir Ashemimry
Busines$ Kids
301 Almeria Ave., Suite 330
Coral Gables, FL 33134
(305) 445–8869

A group of young entrepreneurs is headquartered out of Wichita State University, a state-run school. Founded by Fran Jabara, this is the Association of Collegiate Entrepreneurs (ACE). It holds a wonderful annual conference and college-age entrepreneurs from all over the world attend. They publish several newsletters as well.

ACE
Devlin Hall
Wichita State University
1845 N. Fairmount
Wichita, KS 67208
(316) 689–3000

An outgrowth of ACE is a group of young entrepreneurs called Young Entrepreneurs' Organization (YEO), founded by Verne Harnish.

YEO
3011 Chesapeake Ave., N.W.
Washington, DC 20008
(202) 364–3011

BANKS

A close and sympathetic relationship with a commercial bank can be very helpful to a small family enterprise, not only in facilitating loans but also in securing valuable business advice.

Any information you might need on the status of the banking industry is available from the American Bankers Association, a trade organization with about 14,000 members.

American Bankers Association
1120 Connecticut Ave., N.W.
Washington, DC 20036
(202) 663–5000

The Independent Bankers Association is another good trade organization working with banks that help small businesses.

Independent Bankers Association
P.O. Box 267
1168 S. Main St.
Sauk Center, MN 56378
(612) 352–6546

The predominant training organization for commercial lenders is Robert Morris Associates. They provide valuable industry statistics and financial ratios.

Robert Morris Associates
1616 Philadelphia National Bank Building
Broad & Chestnut Sts.
Philadelphia, PA 19107
(215) 665–2858

The widely used Robert Morris Projection of Financial Statements form, for preparing financial statements for business plans, is available from the following source:

Bankers Systems Inc.
P.O. Box 1457
St. Cloud, MN 56302
(612) 251–3060

To cut through some of the red tape involved in getting an SBA guaranteed loan, the SBA has instituted the Preferred Lenders Program (PLP), in which individual banks are granted the authority to make SBA loans. To locate a bank approved by the SBA in the PLP, call the SBA answer desk: (800) 368–5855. (See also Sheshunoff Information Services below.) To check up on the financial health of your bank:

Veribank
P.O. Box 2963
Woburn, MA 01888
(617) 245–8370

How to Get a Business Loan Without Signing Your Life Away is a book, a four-hour videotape and audiotape program by Dr. Joseph R. Mancuso, offering a wealth of information on small business banking.

The Center for Entrepreneurial Management
180 Varick St., Penthouse
New York, NY 10014-4606
(212) 633–0060

Polk's Bank Directory is the most complete source of bank information and bank listings. The North American edition costs $170.

R. L. Polk & Company
2001 Elm Hill Pike
Nashville, TN 37210
(615) 889–3350

The Encyclopedia of Banking and Financing, *Banker and Tradesman*, and *The Commercial Record*, all excellent directories, can be obtained from Bankers Publishing Company.

Bankers Publishing Company
210 South St., 5th floor
Boston, MA 02111
(617) 426–4495

Offshore Banking News offers a free 12-page pamphlet on the benefits of offshore banking.

Jim Straw, Publisher
Offshore Banking News
301 Plymouth Dr., N.E.
Dalton, GA 30720
(404) 259–6035

Veribank, mentioned above, offers information on banking to small business owners, but Sheshunoff offers similar and competitive information. They are frequently used by banks to uncover information on other banks. For $75, they will send you a report analyzing your bank's capital strengths and income performance. With a credit card and a Federal Express account number (or a fax number) you can obtain invaluable in-depth data about any lender.

Sheshunoff Information Services
One Texas Center
505 Barton Springs Rd.
Austin, TX 78704
(512) 472–2244

BOOKS AND RESOURCES

Jossey-Bass Publishers has an excellent family business series entitled the Family Business Series. Various titles, with books appealing primarily to academics.

Jossey-Bass Publishers Inc.
350 Sansome St.
San Francisco, CA 94104-1310
(415) 433–1767

Omnigraphics Inc. publishes sourcebooks and directories that provide a resource for family businesses and the professionals who serve family enterprises. The text, *Family Business Sourcebook,* edited by two of the foremost experts in the field, Dr. Craig E. Aronoff and Dr. John L. Ward. Cost of the text is $85.

Omnigraphics Inc.
Penobscot Building
Detroit, MI 48226
(313) 961–1340

The Family Firm Institute has published its conference proceedings as a two-volume work (see Professional Institutes). The texts are: *Ownership, Control and Family Dynamics*, and *Managing Succession in Family Firms.* They are important resources for practitioners and family business managers. Cost of the set is $75.

Family Firm Institute
Box 476
Johnstown, NY 12095
(518) 762–3853

Gale Research Company publishes a directory of all associations, benefiting all types of businesses, including family enterprises, called *The Encyclopedia of Associations.* Cost is $400 and it is available in regional editions.

Gale Research Company
Book Tower
Detroit, MI 48226
(313) 961–2242
(800) 223–GALE

Working Together: Entrepreneurial Couples, Frank and Sharan Barnett, Ten Speed Press, San Francisco, CA, 1988.

Your Family Business: A Success Guide for Growth and Survival, Benjamin Benson, Dow Jones-Irwin, New York, NY, 1990.

Family Ties, Corporate Bonds, Paula Bernstein, Doubleday, New York, NY, 1985.

Family Business, Risky Business: How to Make It Work, David Bork, AMACOM, New York, NY, 1986.

House of Dreams: The Collapse of an American Dynasty, Marie Brennan, Avon Books, New York, NY, 1988. The story of the Bingham family of Louisville, KY.

Beyond Survival: A Business Owner's Guide for Success, Leon A. Danco, University Press, Cleveland, OH, 1982.

Someday It'll All Be . . . Whose: The Lighter Side of the Family Business, Leon Danco and Donald J. Jonovic, Center for Family Business, Cleveland, OH, 1990.

The Fords: An American Epic, Peter Collier and David Horowitz, Summit Books, New York, NY, 1987.

Family Pride: Profiles of America's Best Run Family Businesses, Thomas Goldwasser, Dodd, Mead & Co., New York, NY, 1986. The story of Johnson Wax, Marriott Noxell, H & R Block, and Hallmark.

Working with the Ones You Love, Dennis Jaffe, Conari Press, Berkeley, CA. 1990.

A Survival Kit for Wives, Don and Renee Martin, Villard Books, New York, NY, 1986.

Gucci: A House Divided, Gerald McKnight, Donald J. Fine Inc., 1987.

In Love and in Business, Sharon Nelton, John Wiley & Sons, New York, NY, 1986.

Sharing the Vision, Nathan Shulman, National Automobile Dealers Association, McLean, VA, 1990.

Inside the Family-Held Business, M. Stern, Harcourt, Brace, New York, NY, 1986.

Keeping the Family Business Healthy, J. Ward, Jossey-Bass, San Francisco, CA, 1987.

Father, Son & Co., Thomas Watson Jr. and Peter Petre, Bantam Books, New York, NY, 1990. The story of IBM.

Business Development Corporations and State Business Development Agencies

The purpose of business development corporations (BDCs) is to attract and retain businesses in their respective states, and thus to increase employment. Although they sound like government agencies, BDCs are *private* organizations that operate within a state. Their shareholders are usually other private financial institutions located within the state, mainly savings banks and insurance companies, although industrial companies are sometimes investors.

Interest rates on BDC loans are usually a function of the prime rate and range from 2 to 4 percent above the prevailing rate. In addition, some BDCs charge application fees and commitment fees. These fees generally do not total more than 1½ percent of the loan. A prime advantage of BDC loans is the longer maturities available. A bank will rarely offer more than five years for a term loan; however, BDC loans have average maturities of between four and ten years.

Although most BDCs require collateral, many will accept second liens. The owners should be prepared to assign key-man life insurance and personally to guarantee the loan if the business is closely held.

BDCs are lenders, not investors, and are usually not interested in equity positions in the business. However, a few, such as the New York Business Development Corporation, have formed small business investment company subsidiaries (SBICs). The SBIC will take equity positions, generally via subordinated debt with warrants (or a convertible feature) to round out a financing package.

BDCs are specifically designed to provide long-term capital to small businesses. For more information, contact your local Chamber of Commerce or the following:

National Association of Business Development Association
Industrial Development Corporation of Florida
801 N. Magnolia Ave., Suite 218
Orlando, FL 32803
(305) 841–2640

National Association of State Development Agencies
444 N. Capitol St., N.W.
Suite 611
Washington, DC 20001
(202) 624–5411
Contact for name and address of your state development agency.

Chamber of Commerce

The U.S. Chamber of Commerce is the largest volunteer business federation in the world. The individuals, companies, associations, and chambers of commerce that it comprises represent all aspects of business in locations throughout the United States. The national headquarters has resources specifically geared for small enterprises.

The Center for Small Business provides issue reports as well as staffing for the Council of Small Business. It is actively involved in representing small business before the government. And, the Small Business Programs, a part of the office of the Chamber of Commerce Relations, provides members with an information exchange, the *Small Business Update,* and other publications.

U.S. Chamber of Commerce
Center for Small Business
1615 H St., N.W.
Washington, DC 20062
(202) 463–5503

The North Central Regional Office serves Illinois, Indiana, Kentucky, Michigan, and Ohio.

U.S. Chamber of Commerce
North Central Regional Office
2000 Spring Rd., Suite 600
Oak Brook, IL 60521
(708) 574–7918

The Eastern Regional Office serves Connecticut, Delaware, Maine, Massachusetts, New Jersey, New Hampshire, New York, Pennsylvania, Rhode Island, and Vermont.

U.S. Chamber of Commerce
Northeastern Regional Office
711 Third Ave., Suite 1702
New York, NY 10017
(212) 370–1440

The Southwestern Regional Office serves Arkansas, Louisiana, Missouri, New Mexico, Oklahoma, and Texas.

U.S. Chamber of Commerce
Southwestern Regional Office
4835 LBJ Freeway, Suite 750
Dallas, TX 75244
(214) 387–0404

The Western Regional Office serves Alaska, Arizona, California, Hawaii, Idaho, Nevada, Oregon, Utah, and Washington.

U.S. Chamber of Commerce
Western Regional Office
500 Airport Blvd., Suite 240
Burlingame, CA 94010
(415) 348–4011

Consultant Services

An association of management consulting firms, composed of two firms that merged (IMC and ACME), provides specialized professional management help and consulting directories.

C.C.O.
230 Park Ave., Suite 544
New York, NY 10169
(212) 697–9693
(800) 221–2557

The American Association of Professional Consultants is a national professional association providing seminars, insurance programs, meetings, and publications on consulting.

Bill Steinhart
American Association of Professional Consultants
9240 Ward Pkwy.
Kansas City, MO 64114
(816) 648–2679

In addition to several good pamphlets on consulting and related subjects, the Small Business Administration (SBA) offers two consulting services for small businesses: The Service Corps of Retired Executives (SCORE) and The Active Corps of Executives (ACE). You should consult your local telephone directory for the regional SBA office nearest you, or contact:

SBA
409 Third St., S.W.
Washington, DC 20416
(202) 653–6881
(800) 368–5855 (hotline)

Time-Place is an on-line database of consulting professionals. Available through subscription database services and the American Society for Training and Development, it accepts advertising from consultants on database.

Time-Place
460 Totten Pond Rd.
Waltham, MA 02154
(617) 890–4636

The Consultants Library offers a large selection of books on consulting as well as a free catalog of listings.

Herbert Bermont
The Consultants Library
1290 Palm Ave.
Sarasota, FL 34236

The Consultants Bookstore provides free catalogs, a directory of executive recruiters, and a monthly newsletter with inside information on the consulting industry, called *Consultants News.*

James Kennedy
Consultants Bookstore
Templeton Rd.
Fitzwilliam, NH 03447
(603) 585–6544 (bookstore)
(603) 585–2200

Widely known as the "consultant's consultant," Howard Shenson offers these materials: books, tapes, seminars, a free resource guide, and a monthly newsletter called *The Professional Consultant.*

Howard Shenson
Howard L. Shenson Inc.
20720 Ventura Blvd., Suite 206
Woodland Hills, CA 91364
(818) 703–1415

Directories of Telephone Numbers, Addresses, and Zip Codes

The telephone company now charges you for every long-distance information call. Using the *National Directory of Addresses and Telephone Numbers* saves money as well as time. It is a real time and money saver, as it lists most frequently called telephone numbers.

Susan Keech
General Information
11715 North Creek, Pkwy. South
Suite 106
Bothel, WA 98011
(206) 483–4555

You may need a second directory of zip codes. I recommend the two-volume Zip Code and Post Office Directory, which costs $30. They also sell telephone area code listings and maps. While this information is sometimes cheaper via the Post Office, NIDC is better organized than the Post Office.

National Information Data Center
P.O. Box 2977
Washington, DC 20013
(301) 565–2539 (general information)
(214) 696–5156 (shipping information)

A complete directory of zip codes (about the size of the Manhattan Yellow Pages) is available from any U.S. Post Office. This is the cheapest ($15) source of zip-code information. Like all government agencies, they use voice mail, and are almost impossible to deal with as a customer.

Superintendent of Documents
Government Printing Office
Washington, DC 20402
(202) 783–3238

The AT & T Consumer and Business Toll-Free Directory has both Yellow and White Pages. The 8½″ × 11″ telephone book costs $10. The business directory is $15.

AT & T 800 Numbers
P.O. Box 44068
Jacksonville, FL 32231
(800) 562–2255 (order line)

AT & T 800 Numbers
Toll-Free Directory
295 N. Maple Ave.
Basking Ridge, NJ 07920
(publisher)
(201) 221–2000

Janan Weber
AT & T
55 Corporate Dr.
Bridgewater, NJ 08807
(201) 658–6000

U.S. Postal Service 1991 zip plus four directories and five-digit zip code directories are each just $12, a great value.

National Five-Digit Zip Code Directory Orders
National Address Information Center
U.S. Postal Service
6060 Primacy Pkwy., Suite 101
Memphis, TN 38188-0001
(800) 238–3150, ext. 680 outside of Tennessee
(800) 233–0453, ext. 640 in Tennessee

EMPLOYEE STOCK OWNERSHIP PROGRAMS

There are many advantages available to entrepreneurs who elect to sell their business to their employees by using employee stock ownership programs (ESOPs). The new tax laws of 1986 strengthen this option even further, although less than 10,000 companies have taken advantage of ESOPs to date. This program was created by lawyer-economist Louis O. Kelso and was sponsored by Russel B. Long, the Democratic senator from Louisiana.

The National Center for Employees Ownership is a nonpolitical association that provides information on ESOPs.

Carey Rosen
Karen Young
National Center for Employee Ownership
2201 Broadway, Suite 807
Oakland, CA 94612
(415) 272–9461

The ESOP Association is an industry trade organization that is active in making ESOPs more attractive via legislation.

David Binns
ESOP Association
1100 17th St., N.W., Suite 1207
Washington, DC 20036
(202) 293–2971

Benefits Concepts Inc. is a group that is very active on the East Coast in establishing ESOPs.

Don Israel
Benefits Concepts Inc.
101 Park Ave., 26th floor
New York, NY 10178
(212) 682–9480

Kelso & Co. are the pioneers in the field.

Louis Kelso
Kelso & Company
505 Sansome St., Suite 1005
San Francisco, CA 94111
(415) 788–7454

ESTATE PLANNING

For life insurance matters for family businesses, we can recommend the following individuals able to handle such issues.

Thomas F. Clark
Cigna
8200 Greensboro Dr.
McLean, VA 22101
(703) 821–1685
(703) 442–0711

John D. Regan
Regan Holding Corporation
199 Petaluma Blvd. North
Petaluma, CA 94952
(707) 778–8638

Leo Thomas
Thomas Financial & Insurance
5900 Wilshire Blvd., No. 17
Los Angeles, CA 90036
(213) 937–8400

Richard L. Kohlhausen
Capitol Risk Management
Services Ltd.
One Water St.
White Plains, NY 10601
(914) 946–7161

Steven H. Dubin
Williams & Dubin Inc.
1266 Furnace Brook Pkwy.
Quincy, MA 02169
(617) 786–1625

John J. Schortmann, Jr.
John J. Schortmann Insurance
1424 Highland Ave.
Needham, MA 02192
(617) 444–7011

Stuart A. Paris
Paris International Corporation
2 Linden Place
Great Neck, NY 11021
(516) 487–2630

Charles Horn
Horn and Herbitter, Inc.
99 Oakfield Avenue
Dix Hills, NY 11746
(212) 687–1030

Family Business Consultants

A leading consultant in the field of family-owned business is management specialist Barbara Hollander. Her consulting focuses on continuity planning.

Dr. Barbara Hollander
Barbara S. Hollander Associates
The Keisling Building
102 Broadway, Suite 400
Carnegie, PA 15106
(412) 276–6651

The DMA Group, primarily established for the automotive industry, offers professional personal consulting and coaching to family-owned businesses.

Richard Caravati
DMA Group
239 Drakeside Rd.
Hampton, NH 03842
(603) 926–8000

A prominent family business consultant and expert on the subject is Nat Shulman, author of the book *Sharing the Vision* (NADA, 1990).

Nat Shulman
Best Chevrolet
128 Derby St.
Hingham, MA 02043
(617) 749–1950

A leading consultant and specialist in management organization, succession, and ownership transition in the successful family-owned business is Dr. Donald J. Jonovic, the founder of Family Business Management Services in Cleveland, Ohio.

Dr. Donald J. Jonovic
Family Business Management Services
P.O. Box 909
Cleveland, OH 44120
(216) 752–7970

A psychologist with extensive family business experience is Bernard Liebowitz.

Liebowitz and Associates
980 North Michigan Ave.
Suite 1400
Chicago, IL 60611-4501
(312) 334–2003

Franchising

Franchising exists in many industries: fast foods, motels, automobiles and parts, infrared heating, business services, dry cleaning, home repair, health clubs, industrial supplies, building products, schools, vending operations, and so on. Although franchise operations are not new, they have expanded greatly since the mid-seventies. Millions of outlets now exist in all fields, accounting for more than $800 billion in annual sales.

A franchising operation is a legal contractual relationship between a franchisor (the company offering the franchise) and a franchisee (the individual who will own the business). Usually the franchisor is obligated to maintain a continuing interest in the business of the franchisee in such areas as site location, management training, financing, marketing, promotion, and record keeping. In addition, the franchisor offers the use of a store motif, standardized operating procedures, prescribed territory, and a trade name. The franchisee, in return, agrees to operate under the conditions set forth by the franchisor. For the help and services provided, the franchisee is usually expected to make a capital investment in the business. In addition, the franchisee agrees to buy all of his products from the franchisor.

Franchising allows a manufacturer to conserve capital and to simultaneously establish a distribution system in the shortest possible time. It takes many dollars and much time to develop a major distribution system. Using franchises may reduce both expenditures because the franchisee finances part of the system through his initial franchise fee and because it is many times easier and faster to enlist independent firms. Also, franchising makes lower marketing costs a possibility for the manufacturer. Franchising substantially cuts down on the subsequent commitment to fixed overhead expenses like personnel administration. For the franchisee, a franchise may facilitate going into business because it cuts down on the amount of capital required and provides a sense of security through the guidance offered by the franchisor. Franchising is a way for small business owners to avoid problems that can ruin a business.

Francorp is an excellent Chicago-based consulting organization. Their book, *The Franchise Advantage,* is excellent for franchisors.

Donald Boroian, Chairman
Pat Boroian, President
20200 Governors Dr.
Olympia Field, IL 60461
(708) 481–2900

The Franchise Consulting Group is a fine group of experts on franchising.

Edward Kushell
The Franchise Consulting Group
2049 Century Park East, Suite 2295
Los Angeles, CA 90067
(213) 552–2901

Contact Pilot Books for a complete list of titles on franchising, including the Directory of Franchising Organizations and Franchise Investigation & Contract Negotiation.

Pilot Books
103 Cooper St.
Babylon, NY 11702
(516) 422–2225

The International Franchise Association offers information on publications on franchising, including the quarterly *Franchising World.* We especially like the publication *The 21 Most Commonly Asked Questions About Franchising.*

William Cherkasky
International Franchise Association (IFA)
1350 New York Ave., N.W., Suite 900
Washington, DC 20005
(202) 628–8000

Entrepreneur magazine offers an annual "Franchising Directory" issue. This is an excellent source of data. Their January 1991 issue has 1,111 franchises listed and rated in a 410-page issue.

Entrepreneur
2392 Morse Ave.
Irvine, CA 92714
(714) 261–2325

The Franchising Opportunities Handbook (1990 edition, order no. 003-008-00201-3), published by the U.S. government, is the most complete reference book of its kind. It gives information on the number of franchise outlets, length of time the franchise has been in business, start-up capital required, and assistance given by franchisors to franchisees. The cost is $15.

Superintendent of Documents
U.S. Government Printing Office
710 N. Capital St., N.E.
Washington, DC 20402-9325
(202) 783–3238

Information Press has published a directory of about 5,000 franchise listings for twenty-two years; they also publish information on Franchise News Inc.

Info Press
728 Center St.
P.O. Box 550
Lewiston, NY 14092-0550
(716) 754–4669

They had 4,185 franchisors, 2,552 of which are in the U.S., 1,185 are in Canada and 450 are overseas.

A guidebook for those interested in buying a franchise, but should be useful to a new franchisor in familiarizing him or her with what prospective franchisees are looking for. Presents information through a series of questions to be asked of franchisors.

Franchise Index/Profile: A Franchise Evaluation Process, C. R. Stigelman, 1986, Small Business Management Series, No. 35, Small Business Administration, Washington, DC 20416. (800) 368–5855.

Government Information

A great deal of information about small businesses is available from the federal government. However, getting that information is sometimes more difficult than tackling the original problem the information was intended to solve. There are a number of organizations and associations that help small business owners. This chapter lists some of the fundamental sources of help. Also, try contacting your local, state, and city governments; the chamber of commerce in each of these areas is especially important. Moreover, state and regional government associations can also provide some of this information.

Information about selling your product overseas or about buying products from overseas markets is equally important. The Yellow Pages of New York City and Los Angeles list most of the import–export offices of major companies. These directories are invaluable.

SBA is the arm of the federal government charged with helping entrepreneurs.

- SBA Hotline: (800) 368–5855
- Small Business Development Center coordinates SBA-sponsored groups: (202) 653–6768
- Financial Assistance includes banks in local areas that are participants in PLP: (202) 653–2585
- SBIR Program coordinates all SBIR grants: (202) 653–6458.

Much of this wealth of information is not used because too few small business owners know about it. The next time you need information or are trying to solve a problem, call the National Referral Service of the Library of Congress at (202) 426–5467; it is a good starting point for most information searches. The Library of Congress routinely conducts searches free of charge and handles most queries in less than five days. The Federal Information Center can direct you to the right government agency to get the information you need; call (202) 755–8660. The Commerce Department's ITA will compile business profiles on your foreign competitors at a cost as low as $25; call (202) 377–2000.

GSA arranges for the purchase of billions of dollars of items that civilian agencies need, such as computers, automobiles, and office supplies. It provides two broad procurement services for small businesses: First, GSA provides specifics on what it is buying and whether individual small businesses might qualify as suppliers; second, it disseminates information and advice on selling to other federal agencies.

Government Services

GSA provides its services through Business Service Centers in each of its thirteen regional offices (Atlanta, Boston, Chicago, Denver, Fort Worth,

Houston, Kansas City, Los Angeles, New York, Philadelphia, San Francisco, Seattle, and Washington, DC). According to a GSA booklet, the centers "exist primarily to serve entrepreneurs in their search for government contracts." For businesses located outside the thirteen metropolitan areas with Business Service Centers, the GSA operates a "Circuit Rider Program"; GSA counselors visit outlying cities periodically.

General Services Administration
18th & F Sts., N.W.
Washington, DC 20405
(202) 501–0800 (head of GSA)
(703) 557–7901 (procuring information)

SBIR offers seed money grants to small businesses for research and development. Phase I grants range between $25,000 and $50,000. Phase II follow-up grants range between $250,000 and $500,000. Grants are administered by eleven different government agencies.

Office of Innovation, Research and Technology
Small Business Administration
409 3rd St., S.W.
Washington, DC 20416
(202) 653–8842

The Office of Business Liaison serves as liaison between the Department of Commerce and the business community. Its free publication, Business Services Directory, is aimed at making the government more accessible to small businesses. Also available is the ROADMAP Program service, which provides information about government procurement, exporting, statistical sources, marketing, and regulatory matters.

Office of Business Liaison
U.S. Department of Commerce
Room 5898C
Washington, DC 20230
(202) 377–3176

There are thirty-seven Federal Information Centers located throughout the United States. Their job is to personally assist the public in using the federal government as a source of information. To find a center near you, check the White Pages of your telephone book under "U.S. Government."

Your congressman's office is a good place to turn to when all else fails. Remember, your congressman works for you in Washington. He/She can be reached by contacting the local district office or by writing to the following address:

c/o U.S. Capitol
House of Representatives
Washington, DC 20515
(202) 224–3121

The Chamber of Commerce is an excellent source of data on both large and small businesses throughout the United States.

Chamber of Commerce USA
1615 H St., N.W.
Washington, DC 20062
(202) 463–5503

SBA's Office of Procurement and Technical Assistance maintains capability profiles on small businesses interested in federal government procurement opportunities. PASS is used by federal agencies and major prime contractors to identify the capabilities of individual small businesses. Appropriate forms for participating in PASS are available from any SBA office, or from the following source.

Diane Thompson
General Information
Procurement Automated Source System (PASS)
Procurement Assistance
Small Business Administration
409 3rd St., N.W.
Washington, DC 20416
(202) 653–6938
(202) 653–6586

SCORE is an organization of retired businesspeople that provides actual or potential entrepreneurs with free advice. It operates an answer desk that provides information on all government agencies: (800) 368–5855.

Service Corps of Retired Executives (SCORE)
1129 20th St., N.W.
Washington, DC 20416
(202) 653–6279

The U.S. Government Printing Office is one of the best sources of information around. For a small fee, you can get many booklets on business management and basics, such as doing business with the Federal Government.

Superintendent of Documents
U.S. Government Printing Office
Washington, DC 20402
(202) 783–3238

For a computer search, call the Federal Domestic Assistance Staff at the General Services Administration [(202) 708–5126] and ask for the access point nearest you.

Office of Energy-Related Inventions
National Institute of Standards and Technology
Gaithersburg, MD 20899
(301) 975–5500
Disburses grants for energy-related inventions.

Overseas Ventures/Export Financing

Contact for loans for overseas ventures and export financing respectively:

Overseas Private Investment Corp.
1615 M St., N.W.
Washington, DC 20527
(800) 424–6742
(202) 457–7010

Export–Import Bank of the United States
811 Vermont Ave., N.W.
Washington, DC 20571
(800) 424–5201
(202) 566–8990

Minorities/Women
U.S. Department of Commerce
Minority Business Development Agency (MBDA)
Information Clearinghouse
(202) 377–1936

Contact for location of local MBDA offices, which provide counseling for small businesses and help find financing.

Non-Government Sources

The Washington Researchers are an excellent source of government information. They offer many books, tapes, and directories that are designed to answer questions about government services and programs.

Washington Researchers
2612 P St., N.W.
Washington, DC 20007-3062
(202) 333–3499

Matthew Lesko, founder of Washington Researchers, has compiled a one-volume guide to "the largest source of information on Earth," the U.S. government. Titled *Information U.S.A.,* this guide provides names, addresses, and phone numbers for more than 3,000 government data experts, as well as access to more than 1 million free and low-cost government publications. The cost is $23 for the softcover edition, $50 for the hardcover edition.

Penguin U.S.A.
120 Woodbine St.
Bergenfield, NJ 07621
(201) 387–0600

The *Small Business Dealers Guide to Selling to the Government,* an 8½″ × 11″ paperback by Joseph T. Foglia, 1989, is excellent for the under $25,000 small business set-asides. It costs $12 from JTF Inc., Box 5521, Virginia Beach, VA 23455.

Government Procurement Assistance Center Inc.
1426 Davis Ford Road
Woodbridge, VA 22192
(703) 643–1072.

A clearinghouse of procurement information. Bills itself as an "affordable" alternative for small firms. Available on annual subscription basis with prices ranging from $900 to $2,500.

Contract Opportunities
577 Merritt Ave.
Oakland, CA 94610
(415) 444–4909.

Helps design marketing plans and strategies for securing government contracts and corporate subcontracts.

Eagle Eye Publishers

This company has crammed information on 400,000 federal contracts onto a single CD-ROM computer disk. The $2,650 price tag may scare you, but it includes a CD-ROM drive to hook up to your computer. Contact Eagle Eye at 10 W. Washington St., Middleburg, VA 22117 (703) 687–6777.

Helpful Publications

Doing Business with the Federal Government
$2.50 from Consumer Information Center, Dept. 110-W, Pueblo, CO 81008. Booklet on how to bid on government contracts and market to federal agencies.

Commerce Business Daily
$261 a year first-class postage from Superintendent of Documents, Government Printing Office, Washington, DC 20402 (202) 783–3238. Lists RFPs, contract awards, other key data.

United States Government Manual
$21 from the Government Printing Office (address and phone above). Lists agencies, key executives, field offices, sources of information, and functions of principal subagencies.

U.S. Government Purchasing and Sales Directory
$16 from Government Printing Office. Products and services purchased by various agencies.

Small Business Subcontracting Directory
Free from SDBU offices at various government agencies or from Office of Procurement Assistance, SBA, 1441 L St. N.W., Washington, DC 20416. Major government contractors that subcontract to small businesses.

Federal Executive Directory
$155 (plus $15 shipping) annual subscription for six updates from Carroll Publishing Co., 1058 Thomas Jefferson St. N.W., Washington DC 20007 (202) 333–8620. Over 87,000 entries. Single copy is $105 plus $4 shipping.

Home-Based Businesses

Millions of Americans are finding that there is no place like home to work. It not only cuts down on commuting time but it also offers a number of financial incentives. Recent estimates indicated that there are more than 14 million home-based businesses in the United States. As a result, a number of associations, newsletters, and books have sprung up to help the home-based entrepreneur.

Associations

The American Home Business Association is a very new association for home-based business owners and operators. It publishes *Home Business Line,* a monthly newsletter.

American Home Business Association
397 Post Rd.
Darien, CT 06820
(203) 655–4380
(800) 433–6361

A division of the Small-Business Development Center, the Center for Home-Based Businesses is a clearinghouse for information on home-based businesses. It offers "Organizations for Home-Based Business," a comprehensive list of organizations of interest to home businesses.

Leslie McDonald
Center for Home-Based Businesses
Truman College
1145 W. Wilson
Chicago, IL 60640
(312) 989–6112

Founded in 1982, the National Association for the Cottage Industry acts as an advocacy system for cottage workers. This 30,000-member group publishes a bimonthly newsletter, *Mind Your Own Business at Home,* also publishes the Kern Reports on trends in home-based businesses, and holds two meetings a year.

Betty Fifer
National Association for the Cottage Industry
P.O. Box 14460
Chicago, IL 60614
(312) 472–8116

The National Association of Home-Based Businesses was founded in 1984. This 3,000-member group holds an annual meeting and offers a number of publications on operating a home-based business.

Cynthia Brower
National Association of Home-Based Businesses
P.O. Box 362
Owings Mills, MD 21117
(301) 363–3698

Home Business News is a bimonthly magazine for home-based entrepreneurs; it features articles on marketing, mail order, and computers.

Home Business News
12221 Beaver Pike
Jackson, OH 45640
(614) 988–2331

Mothers' Home Business Network is a group of 5,000 members who publish a networking newsletter for mothers who work at home.

Georganne Fiumara
Mothers' Home Business Network
P.O. Box 423
East Meadow, NY 11554
(516) 997–7394

Barbara Brabec Productions publishes *National Home Business Report,* a quarterly newsletter that contains a wide range of information and advice on operating a home business. Also available is *Homemade Money: The Definitive Guide to Success in a Home Business,* by Barbara Brabec. The cost is $16.45 postpaid.

National Home Business Report
Barbara Brabec Productions
P.O. Box 2137
Naperville, IL 60566
(Requests for information by mail only)
(708) 717–0488

Starting and Managing a Business from Your Home is a 48-page booklet from SBA, which discusses the pluses and minuses of home-based businesses, including how to get started, record keeping, taxes, and pertinent laws. The cost is $1.75.

Starting and Managing a Business from Your Home
Department 146-R
Consumer Information Center
Pueblo, CO 81009

Incorporating and Forming Partnerships

One of the first steps in setting up a business is to decide the form it will take: sole proprietorship, general partnership, limited partnership, or corporation.

How to Incorporate for Under $75.00 Without a Lawyer, by Ted Nicholas, is worthwhile reading for anyone considering incorporation. This is an excellent source of forms, books, and quasilegal information. Enterprise Publishing can also provide forms for incorporation in any of the fifty states.

Ted Nicholas
Enterprise Publishing Company
725 Market St.
Wilmington, DE 19801
(302) 654–0110
(800) 533–2665

Investigate the benefits of incorporating in the state of Delaware. *Incorporating in Delaware*, published by the Guage Corporation, is an informative booklet which lists the advantages of Delaware incorporation and all of the forms necessary for setting up a Delaware corporation. The cost is $5. They are a P.R. firm promoting Delaware as a good state in which to do business.

Guage Corporation
1300 N. Market St., Suite 501
Wilmington, DE 19801
(302) 658–8045

The Partnership Book: How to Write Your Own Small Business Partnership Agreement, 3rd edition (revised to cover new tax rules), was written by Dennis

Clifford and Ralph Warner. Nolo Press also offers books for many state incorporations. This is an excellent source of legal help for entrepreneurs.

Nolo Press
950 Parker St.
Berkeley, CA 94710
(415) 549–1976
(415) 548–5902 (fax)
(800) 640–6656 (in California)
(800) 992–6656 (outside California)

Corporate Agents, Inc., a group of corporate register agents, will provide information on how to incorporate in Delaware.

Corporate Agents, Inc.
P.O. Box 1281
Wilmington, DE 19899
(800) 441–4303
(302) 998–0598

Delaware Business Incorporators will help you to incorporate in Delaware and then help you to file to do business in your home state.

Lori M. Smith, General Manager
Delaware Business Incorporators
3422 Old Capitol Trail, Suite 700
Wilmington, DE 19808
(800) 423–2993
(302) 996–5819

If you want to purchase a corporate kit and stock certificates (including seal and by-laws) and don't want to pay a lawyer to do it for you, go directly to their source, the Corpex Bank Note Company, Inc.

Corpex Bank Note Co., Inc.
480 Canal St.
New York, NY 10013
(212) 925–2400
(800) 221–8181 (outside New York)
(800) 522–7299 (in New York)

INCUBATORS

In brief, incubators, which are most often run by nonprofit corporations, are designed to help start-ups get off the ground by providing low rent, business and financial advice (including advice on business plans and SBA loans), as well as secretarial and computer services. Moreover, studies show that start-ups in incubators fail only 50 percent of the time, compared with an 80-percent failure rate for businesses started on the outside.

Associations

An industry trade association for incubators, the National Business Incubation Association is very effective in helping areas with high unemployment to create new business centers.

Dinah Adkins
National Incubation Association
One President St.
Athens, OH 45701
(614) 593–4331

Miscellaneous Services

David Allen is a good source of incubator information.

Dr. David Allen
501 "D" Business Administration Building
Penn State University
University Park, PA 16802
(814) 865–0580

Mark Weinberg is an expert in urban incubators.

Dr. Mark Weinberg
Institute for Local Government and Rural Development
67 Bentley Hall
Ohio University
Athens, OH 45701
(614) 593–4388

John Mullen is an expert in rural incubators.

Dr. John Mullen
Landscape Architecture
University of Massachusetts
109 Hills-North
Amherst, MA 01003
(413) 545–2255

Incubators Times, a quarterly newsletter published by SBA, keeps entrepreneurs up-to-date on the activities of business incubators around the United States.

Office of Private Initiatives
Small Business Administration
409 3rd St., S.W.
Washington, DC 20416
(202) 653–7880

LEGAL SERVICES

Used for a wide range of conflicts, including construction warranties, dissolution of partnerships, cost overruns, and consumer complaints, the American Arbitration Association offers a good alternative to the court process.

American Arbitration Association
140 W. 51st St.
New York, NY 10020
(212) 484–4000

The American Bar Association maintains a legal referral service.

American Bar Association
750 N. Lake Shore Dr.
Chicago, IL 60611
(312) 988–5000

Listed below are several lawyers competent in family business matters who can be referred to as sources of help.

Dennis O'Connor
O'Connor, Bourde, Snyder & Aronson
950 Winter St., Suite 2300
Waltham, MA 02154
(617) 890–6600

Gerald Tishler
Brown, Rudnick, Freed & Gesmer
One Financial Center, 18th floor
Boston, MA 02111
(617) 330–9000

Karen Carasik
Much, Selist, Freed, Denenberg
Ament & Elger, P.C.
200 N. LaSalle St.
Suite 2100
Chicago, IL 60601-1095
(312) 346–3100
(312) 621–1436

Roger Boyle
Boyle, Vogeler & Haimes
30 Rockefeller Plaza
New York, NY 10112
(212) 265–5100

T. Michael Wilson
Jackson & Walker
901 Main St., 60th floor
Dallas, TX 75202
(214) 953–6020

Thomas L. Watters
Hart, Jakle & Watters
12400 Wilshire Blvd.
Suite 450
Los Angeles, CA 90025
(213) 826–5202

Edward Gelfand
Barry Friedman
Friedman & Phillips
10920 Wilshire Blvd.
Suite 650
Los Angeles, CA 90024-6508
(213) 208–2889

Mergers and Acquisitions

Resources

The Institute of Certified Business Counselors is an association of business brokers that assists family enterprise expansion and development.

W. R. Stabbert
Institute of Certified Business Counselors
3485 W. First Ave.
Eugene, OR 97402
(503) 345–8064
(415) 945–8440

The International Association of Merger and Acquisition Consultants (IMAC) are specialists with expertise in medium-sized businesses. They maintain a database on all buyer/seller listings and publish a monthly newsletter.

INTERMAC
200 S. Frontage Rd.
Suite 103
Burr Ridge, IL 60521
(708) 323–0233

The twenty-two-chapter Association for Corporate Growth is concerned with mergers and acquisitions, including family businesses. This is a very effective group for planning departments of larger businesses and business development officers.

Carl Wangman
Executive Director
Association for Corporate Growth
104 Wilmot Rd.
Deerfield, IL 60015
(312) 940–8800

Geneva Business Services, with offices throughout the United States, conducts seminars and provides information on buying and selling businesses. They also arrange for purchase and/or sale of family businesses.

Richard Rodnick
Geneva Business Services
5 Park Plaza
Irvine, CA 92714
(714) 966–2700

A good resource magazine on mergers and acquisitions is *Mergers and Acquisitions,* which helps keep one current on emerging issues in the marketplace. Annual subscription rate is $269.

M.L.R. Publishing
Mergers and Acquisitions
Rittenhouse Square
229 S. 18th St., 3rd floor
Philadelphia, PA 19103
800–MERGING

Specialists

Of those in the area of mergers and acquisitions with some expertise in family business matters, we can recommend the following:

John York
Robert E. Lend Co., Inc.
One N. LaSalle St.
Chicago, IL 60602
(312) 346–2111

Henry S. James
Corporate Finance Associates of North California, Inc.
344 Village Square
Orinoa, CA 94563
(415) 254–9126

Gordon Ness
Computer Tek Ventures
2228 S. El Camino Real
Suite 175
San Mateo, CA 94403
(415) 595–0961

Frank Braje
The Erin Group
509 Aurora Ave.
Naperville, IL 60540
(708) 305–0814

John C. Dealey
Dealey Ltd.
311 N. Market, Suite 203
Dallas, TX 75202
(214) 748–2500

Richard Caravati
DMA Group
239 Drakeside Rd.
Hampton, NH 03842
(603) 926–8000

Robert Collings
RFC Associates
137 Barton Rd.
Stow, MA 01775
(508) 562–9182

Professional Institutes

The dean of professional institutes is the Center for Family Business. Founded by the "grandfather" of family business, Dr. Leon Danco and his wife Katy, the Center has offered books, seminars, and resources on the subject for over twenty years.

Dr. Leon Danco
The Center for Family Business
P.O. Box 24268
Cleveland, OH 44124
(216) 442–0800
(216) 442–0178 (fax)

The Family Firm Institute is an independent interdisciplinary organization dedicated to supporting practice and research in family-owned businesses. It's a trade association of practitioners in the field of family business. Providing a wide range of resources to help answer the needs of today's family-run businesses, it sponsors a leading quarterly journal, *Family Business Review.* Its members are some of the better consultants in this field.

Roderick W. Correll
Executive Director
Chloe Correll
Membership Director
The Family Firm Institute
P.O. Box 476
Johnstown, NY 12095
(518) 762–3853

The National Family Business Council is a private research and consulting group serving family businesses throughout the world. Its primary mission is to help resolve family issues directly affecting family businesses. It also is a resource for speakers on the subject.

John Messervey
Executive Director
National Family Business Council
60 Revere Dr., Suite 500
Northbrook, IL 60062
(708) 480–9574

The Midwest Association of Family Business Owners is a professional organization that helps network family businesses.

Director
Midwest Association of Family Business Owners
P.O. Box 261
Hinsdale, IL 60522-0261
(708) 323–2460

The Independent Business Institute is a major resource on family businesses, providing information and consulting services. It also publishes books and special reports for family firms.

Frank Butrick
Managing Director
Independent Business Institute
P.O. Box 1048
Norton, OH 44205
(216) 825–8258

A national Canadian organization that provides resources for family businesses is the Canadian Association of Family Enterprises (CAFE). It also has an excellent newsletter called *Family Enterprising*.

Canadian Association of Family Enterprises
45 St. Clair Ave. W., Suite 602
Toronto, Ontario M4V 1K9
Canada

PUBLICATIONS: JOURNALS, MAGAZINES, AND NEWSLETTERS

A national magazine consistently offering the best material and information on family business subjects is a publication of the Chamber of Commerce called *Nation's Business.* It reaches some 850,000 readers monthly. Columns and articles on this topic are authored by Sharon Nelton, a widely respected writer on family business matters. Her recent text, *How Entrepreneurial Couples Are Changing the Roles of Business and Marriage* (John Wiley & Sons), is excellent.

Sharon Nelton
Nation's Business
1615 H St., N.W.
Washington, DC 20062
(202) 463–5650

A leading magazine on family business is a monthly called *Family Business.* It is widely respected and read, offering a discount program for multiple subscriptions. Subscription rate is $39.97 per year.

Leonard Zweig, Publisher
Steve Solomon, Editor
Rittenhouse Square
229 S. 18th St.
Philadelphia, PA 19103
(215) 790–7000

The Family Business Review is a major quarterly professional magazine sponsored by the Family Firm Institute (see Professional Institutes). It offers professionals working in the area of family business consulting resource information to answer the needs of family businesses. Subscription rates are $48 per year.

Ivan Lansberg, Editor
Family Business Review
Jossey-Bass Inc., Publisher
350 Sansome St.
San Francisco, CA 94104
(415) 433–1767 (orders)
(415) 433–1740 (editorial)

A newsletter devoted to aspects of family business management and development is the quarterly *The Family Business.* It is devoted to the interests of the family-owned business executive. Annual subscription rates are $40, a single issue is $12.50. Dr. Peter Davis is head of the editorial board and Ken Catanella of Shearson is the director.

Shearson Lehman Hutton
Senior Consulting Organization
1600 Market St.
Suite 1300
Philadelphia, PA 19103
(215) 665–3500
(800) 759–4888

A newsletter expected to premier in early 1991 is to be called *Entrepreneurial Couples.* It's for partners in business and marriage.

Larry Isreal & Associates
1625 Olympic Blvd.
Santa Monica, CA 90404
(213) 450–8563

A biweekly newsletter, *Work and Family Connection,* appeals primarily to larger businesses. Rather than being a family business publication, it tells large companies how to be more family-oriented.

Susan Bonoff
Work & Family Connections, Inc.
5197 Beachside Dr., Box 11
Minnetonka, MN 55343
(612) 936–7898

Small Business Answer Desk Directory

Finding the answer to a small business question can mean searching through a maze of federal, state, and private sector information sources. In October 1982, in an effort to assist small business owners and prospective entrepreneurs with their business questions, SBA's Office of Advocacy established a toll-free hotline, the Small Business Answer Desk.

In the course of responding to more than 200,000 inquiries, the Answer Desk staff has developed several tools to aid small business owners in their information search. One of these is the Small Business Answer Desk Directory, which includes lists of key federal and state agencies that provide help to businesses, a list of business and trade organizations, and a glossary of small business terms and programs.

I believe this compilation will be especially useful to members of the small business community. The Small Business Answer Desk is open for telephone inquiries on weekdays from 9:00 A.M. to 5:00 P.M. E.S.T.; call (800) 368–5855.

Office of the Chief Council for Advocacy
Small Business Administration
409 3rd St., S.W.
Washington, DC 20416
(202) 653–7561 (in Washington, DC)
(800) 368–5855

Sources of Small Business Information

In this category, you'll find fundamental organizations designed to help small businesses as well as difficult-to-classify sources. This category is more than a reference: Each source listed may be of value to your business, helping you to solve an immediate problem or to prevent a future problem.

General Sources

The Small Business Reporter is a series of more than 100 pamphlets on small business subjects, which are offered for a small postage and handling charge. A free Publications Index is available from the following source.

Small Business Reporter
Bank of America
P.O. Box 37000, Dept. 3631
San Francisco, CA 94137
(415) 953–7495
(415) 622–3456 (general)

The Center for Entrepreneurial Management is a worldwide, nonprofit association of about 3,000 entrepreneurs. CEM publishes the *Entrepreneurial Manager,* a monthly newsletter, and sells more than 100 books and tapes on the subjects of entrepreneurship and small business management.

Center for Entrepreneurial Management, Inc.
Joseph R. Mancuso, President
180 Varick St., Penthouse
New York, NY 10014-4606
(212) 633–0060

American Express has a new Small Business Partnership and offers an increasing number of financial services to small businesses.

American Express/I.D.S.
900 IDS Tower, Unit 409
Minneapolis, MN 55474
(612) 372–2236

Founded in 1975, the Entrepreneurship Institute is a nonprofit corporation that helps local communities pool their resources to help benefit small businesses. Their locally funded Entrepreneurship Forums provide entrepreneurs with information on state and local programs, as well as networking opportunities.

Jan Zupnick
Entrepreneurship Institute
3592 Corporate Dr., Suite 101
Columbus, OH 43229
(614) 895–1153

Mark Stevens is one of the best writers in the field of small business. His books are both helpful and informative.

Mark Stevens
15 Breckinridge Rd.
Chappaqua, NY 10514
(914) 238–3569

University Programs

A major academic program on family business is at Kennesaw State College in Marietta, Georgia, called the Family Business Forum. Headed by Dr. Craig E. Aronoff, a leading expert in the field of family business, it offers an annual $1,000 membership fee per family company for seminars and networking. It also publishes an excellent quarterly newsletter, *The Family Business Forum Quarterly.*

Dr. Craig E. Aronoff
Kennesaw State College
School of Business Administration
Box 444
Marietta, GA 30061
(404) 423–6045

A leading Midwest academic program for large family businesses is offered by Loyola University of Chicago. Headed by noted scholar and prominent lecturer in the field, Dr. John L. Ward, it offers a program for family businesses to explore through communal family seminars, courses, testing and counseling, and networking. Extensive library resources are available.

Dr. John L. Ward, Director
Loyola University
Family Business Program
One E. Pearson St.
Chicago, IL 60611
(708) 475–3000

Oregon State University offers a networking family business service and program of conferences called The Family Business Network, headed by Pat Frishkoff. It serves as an educational and informational resource to family businesses. It publishes an excellent eighteen-page Family Business Survival Checklist. There is an annual company membership fee of $1,000.

Pat Frishkoff, Director
Family Business Program/Network
Oregon State University
Bexell 205
Corvallis, OR 97331-2603
(503) 737–3326

The Wharton School of the University of Pennsylvania offers a major program on Family Business Studies, headed by Peter Davis. In addition, the school maintains individual courses and resources at the Family Business Center and Aresty Institute of Executive Education.

Peter Davis, Director
Div. of Family Business Studies
The Wharton School of Business
Philadelphia, PA 19104
(215) 898–6848

and

Ian McMillian, Director
Bernie Tannenbaum,
Assoc. Director
Family Business Center
Wharton School of Business
Snider Entrepreneurial Center
3620 Locust Walk
Steinberg-Dietrich Hall
Philadelphia, PA 19104
(215) 898–4856 (general)
(215) 898–1278 (direct)

Baylor University in Waco, Texas, also maintains an Institute for Family Business open to any family business. Headed by Nancy Bowman-Upton, it offers workshops, conferences, and case studies. Fees for the program are $395 for the first family member and $250 for all other family members. The school also has an extensive library on business enterprise.

Prof. Nancy Bowman-Upton
Institute for Family Business
Baylor University
The John F. Baugh Center for Entrepreneurship
BU Box 8011
Waco, TX 76798-8011
(817) 755–2265

VENTURE CAPITAL

Associations

The National Association of Small Business Investment Companies is an association of about 700 SBICs. It publishes a monthly newsletter and sponsors an excellent annual conference on venture capital. A membership directory is available for a $1 handling charge (request in writing only).

National Association of Small Business Investment Companies
1156 15th St., N.W., Suite 1101
Washington, DC 20005
(202) 833–8230

The Heartland Venture Capital Network is a network for Midwest-based firms and investors.

Heartland Venture Capital Network
1840 Oak Ave.
Evanston, IL 60201
(708) 864–7970

The National Venture Capital Association is a loose federation of about 230 venture capital sources. Its membership directory is free on request.

National Venture Capital Association
1655 N. Fort Myer Dr., Suite 700
Arlington, VA 22209
(703) 528–4370

The Western Association of Venture Capitalists offers a free directory of 130 members.

Western Association of Venture Capitalists
3000 San Hill Rd., Building 2, Suite 215
Menlo Park, CA 94025
(415) 854–1322

Miscellaneous Services

Investors register for one year for a $200 fee. Entrepreneurs register for six months for a $200 fee. Entrepreneurs file a three-page summary of their business plans. Mr. Murphy also publishes a newsletter, *The California Technology Stock Letter.*

Michael Murphy
Venture Capital Connection
1620 Montgomery St., Suite 200
San Francisco, CA 94111
(415) 982–0120

For a $55 fee, the Venture Capital Hotline will give you up to ten venture capital sources from its data bank.

Lance J. Strauss
Venture Capital Hotline
26135 Carmel Rancho Blvd., Suite 16
Carmel, CA 93923
(800) 237–2380
(408) 625–0700

The Venture Capital Network is a nonprofit corporation. This unique service matches entrepreneurs needing capital with venture capital sources. Investors register for one year for a $200 fee. Entrepreneurs register for six months for a $100 fee. A faculty member of the University of New Hampshire, Bill Wetzel knows of other similar services across the country. In fact, he is assisting nine other regional centers to become "angel" networks.

Angel Networks

Technology Capital Network
MIT Enterprise Forum
201 Vassar St.
Cambridge, MA 02139
(617) 253–8240

Venture Capital Network of New York, Inc.
(518) 434–5555

Canada Opportunities Investment Network
Ontario Chamber House
2323 Yonge St., 5th floor
Toronto, Ontario M4P2C9
Canada
(800) 387–8943 (in Canada)

Upper Peninsula VCN
1500 Wilkinson Ave.
Marquette, MI 49855
(906) 227–2406

Wyoming Investor Network
Wyoming Small Business Development Center Network
111 W. Second St., Suite 416
Casper, WY 82601
(307) 235–4825

Mid-Atlantic Investment Network
Dingman Center for Entrepreneurship
College of Business & Management
University of Maryland
College Park, MD 20742
(301) 405–2144

Iowa Venture Capital Network
Box 127
Atlantic, IA 50022
(712) 243–3431

Greater Houston Partnership
Economic Development Division
1100 Milam, 25th floor
Houston, TX 77002
(713) 651–7220

Texas Capital Network
8716 N. Mopac Blvd.
Suite 200
Austin, TX 78759
(512) 794–9398

Private Investor Network
University of South Carolina at Aiken
171 University Pkwy.
Aiken, SC 29801
(803) 648–6851 (x3342)

Nebraska VCN
University of Nebraska
1313 Farnham, Suite 132
Omaha, NE 68182–0423
(402) 595–2381

Tennessee VCN
Middle Tennessee State University
Murfreesboro, TN 37132
(615) 898–2100

Washington Investment Network
2001 Sixth Ave.
Suite 2700
Seattle, WA 98121
(206) 464–6282

Northwest Capital Network
P.O. Box 6650
Portland, OR 97228–6650
(503) 294–0643

Pacific VCN
Room 210
Graduate School of Management
University of California at Irvine
Irvine, CA 92717
(714) 856–8366

VCN of Minnesota
Small Business Development Center
23 Empire Dr.
St. Paul, MN 55103
(612) 223–8663

Georgia Capital Network
ATDC
430 Tenth St., Suite N-116
Atlanta, GA 30318
(404) 894–2376

Investment Capital Network
Capital Plaza Tower
Room 2406-OBT
Frankfort, KY 40601
(502) 564–4886

Southwest VCN, Inc.
P.O. Box 44
Goodyear, AZ 85338–0020
(602) 386–6428

Seed Capital Network has about 600 members in the United States.

Seed Capital Network, Inc.
8905 Kingston Pike
Knoxville, TN 37923
(615) 693–2091

Small Business Investment Companies

The Investment Division of the Small Business Administration keeps a directory of all operating SBICs, which is updated every six months. Free.

Investment Division
Small Business Administration
Washington, DC 20416
(202) 653–2806

National Association of Investment Companies publishes a directory of 150 member venture capital firms (mostly SBICs). Send $3.65.

National Association of Investment Companies
1111 14th St., N.W., Suite 700
Washington, DC 20005
(202) 289–4336

David Silver claims to have raised more capital than anyone in the world. His Silver Press is a wonderful source of books and information, including who's who in venture capital.

A. David Silver
The Silver Press
524 Camino Del Monte Sol
Santa Fe, NM 87501
(505) 983–3868

A source of information on venture capital clubs around the world, the International Venture Capital Institute, Inc. publishes a directory and a newsletter. There are about 100 clubs in the United States and another dozen or so overseas.

Carroll Greathouse
The International Venture Capital Institute, Inc.
P.O. Box 1333
Stamford, CT 06904
(203) 323–3143

Publications

Stanley Pratt's *Guide to Venture Capital Sources* is the most valuable venture capital guide available today. His firm, Venture Economics (formerly Capital Publishing), also publishes a valuable venture capital and leveraged buyout newsletter.

Stanley Pratt
Venture Economics, Inc.
75 2nd Ave., Suite 700
Needham, MA 02194
(617) 449–2100

WOMEN ENTREPRENEURS

Women are emerging as a major force in the entrepreneurial world, and organizations and publications are springing up to help them.

Associations

A nonprofit group of women in business, the American Women's Economic Development Corporation has more than 2,000 members nationwide. Services offered include counseling, networking sessions, conferences, lectures, and training programs.

Beatrice Fitzpatrick
American Woman's Economic Development Corporation
60 E. 42nd St., Suite 405
New York, NY 10165
(212) 692–9100
(800) 222–2933 (out of state)
(800) 442–2933 (in NY state)

The Committee of 200 is a 200-member network of high-powered entrepreneurial and corporate women. Services offered include spring and fall conferences, a newsletter, and regional meetings.

Lydia Lewis
Committee of 200
676 North St. Clair, Suite 1900
Chicago, IL 60611
(312) 280–5200

The Interagency Commission on Women's Business Enterprise works to obtain federal contracts for women-owned businesses and to get a larger share of SBA loans to women. Educational programs and counseling for women's start-up companies are also provided.

Interagency Commission on Women's Business Enterprise
SBA's Office of Women in Business
Office of the Chief Counsel for Advocacy
Small Business Administration
Washington, DC 20416
(202) 653–6087
(202) 653–4000

An 800-member organization consisting predominantly of black women, The National Association of Black Women Entrepreneurs is open to women of all races. Services offered include monthly workshops, networking sessions, and a newsletter.

Marilyn Hubbard
National Association of Black Women Entrepreneurs
P.O. Box 1375
Detroit, MI 48231
(313) 341–7400

The National Association of Female Executives is a nonprofit organization with 250,000 members. Services offered include networking and discounts on car rentals, airlines, and so on. *The Female Executive* is published six times a year.

National Association of Female Executives
127 W. 24th St.
New York, NY 10011
(212) 645–0770

The National Association of Women Business Owners is a dues-based national organization that represents women in all types of businesses. It sponsors "Mega-Marketplace," an annual convention that brings women entrepreneurs together with government agencies, private corporations, and banks. They have forty-three chapters nationwide.

Natalie Holmes
National Association of Women Business Owners
600 S. Federal St., Suite 400
Chicago, IL 60605
(312) 922–0465
(708) 655–0081

An independent, nonprofit organization, the Women's Business Development Center serves as a clearinghouse for business information. It provides information on creative financing and conducts broad-based economic development research. Training programs, conferences, workshops, and trade shows are sponsored.

Attn: Alert
The Women's Business Development Center
77 Columbia St.
Albany, NY 12207
(518) 465–5579

U.S. Department of Commerce
Minority Business Development Agency
Information Clearinghouse
(202) 377–1936

Contact for location of local MBDA offices, which provides counseling for small businesses and helps find financing.

National Women's Business Counsel
1441 L St., N.W., Room 414
Washington, DC 20416
(202) 653–8080

Call for information on public and private sector programs (some provide financial assistance) for women business owners. Plans to issue a report by early next year.

The Women's Economic Development Corporation serves 500 active clients; fees are adjusted based on service provided and ability to pay. Services offered include training seminars, individual counseling, and a revolving loan fund for clients.

Kathy Keely
Women's Economic Development Corporation
2324 University Ave., West, Suite 200
St. Paul, MN 55114
(612) 646-3808

Other books by Joseph R. Mancuso published by Prentice Hall Press:

- *How to Prepare and Present a Business Plan*. (ISBN 0-13-425125-3)
- *How to Start, Finance, and Manage Your Own Small Business*. (ISBN 0-13-425133-4)
- *How to Write a Winning Business Plan*. (ISBN 0-13-425141-5)
- *Mancuso's Small Business Resource Guide*. (ISBN 0-13-551888-1)
- *How to Get a Business Loan (Without Signing Your Life Away)*. (ISBN 0-13-407280-4)
- *Buying a Business (For Very Little Cash)* co-authored with Douglas D. Germann. (ISBN 0-13-109521-8)

All of these titles are available at your local bookseller. If you are unable to find these or any other Prentice Hall Press books, please ask your bookseller to order them for you.

Index